Cambridge E<

Elements in the Philosophy of Religion

RELIGIOUS EPISTEMOLOGY

Tyler Dalton McNabb
Houston Baptist University

CAMBRIDGE
UNIVERSITY PRESS

CAMBRIDGE
UNIVERSITY PRESS

University Printing House, Cambridge CB2 8BS, United Kingdom

One Liberty Plaza, 20th Floor, New York, NY 10006, USA

477 Williamstown Road, Port Melbourne, VIC 3207, Australia

314–321, 3rd Floor, Plot 3, Splendor Forum, Jasola District Centre,
New Delhi – 110025, India

79 Anson Road, #06–04/06, Singapore 079906

Cambridge University Press is part of the University of Cambridge.

It furthers the University's mission by disseminating knowledge in the pursuit of
education, learning, and research at the highest international levels of excellence.

www.cambridge.org
Information on this title: www.cambridge.org/9781108457538
DOI: 10.1017/9781108558365

First published 2019

A catalogue record for this publication is available from the British Library.

ISBN 978-1-108-45753-8 Paperback
ISSN 2399-5165 (online)
ISSN 2515-9763 (print)

Religious Epistemology

Elements in the Philosophy of Religion

DOI: 10.1017/9781108558365
First published online: November 2018

Tyler Dalton McNabb
Houston Baptist University

Abstract: If epistemology is roughly the study of knowledge, justification, warrant, and rationality, then religious epistemology is the study of how these epistemic concepts relate to religious belief and practice. This Element, while surveying various religious epistemologies, argues specifically for Plantingian religious epistemology. It makes the case for proper functionalism and Plantinga's AC models, while it also responds to debunking arguments informed by cognitive science of religion. It serves as a bridge between religious epistemology and natural theology.

Keywords: religious epistemology, Plantinga, cognitive science, Proper Functionalism

ISBNs: 9781108457538 (PB), 9781108558365 (OC)
ISSNs: 2399-5165 (online), 2515-9763 (print)

Contents

1 Religious Epistemology

1.1 Religious Epistemology

If epistemology is roughly the study of knowledge, though more broadly understood also as the study of justification, warrant, and rationality, religious epistemology is the study of how these epistemic concepts relate to religious belief and practice. Broadly speaking, this Element is about religious epistemology. More specifically, though, in this Element I argue for a specific religious epistemology. Roughly, I argue for the plausibility of Plantingian religious epistemology. I take Plantingian religious epistemology to be made up of two specific tenets. The first tenet is proper functionalism. At the heart of proper functionalism is the thesis that a belief can be warranted if it is the product of properly functioning faculties. The second tenet is Reformed epistemology. Reformed epistemology is the thesis that religious belief can be justified or warranted apart from argument. There are some epistemological views that are compatible with the thesis of Reformed epistemology but are not within the family of proper functionalism. In fact, I take it that almost all mainstream epistemological theories are compatible with the thesis of Reformed epistemology[1]. I will mention such theories in this section. Before I do this, however, I will entertain one specific epistemological theory that is not compatible with either of Plantinga's tenets. This theory is best known as classical foundationalism. After giving arguments against this view, I will move on to discussing the epistemological theories that are compatible with the thesis of Reformed epistemology. This will set up Section 2. There I will argue specifically for the thesis of proper functionalism and discuss how Plantinga utilizes it to argue for the thesis of Reformed epistemology. This will give the reader reasons to prefer Plantinga's articulation of Reformed epistemology over the articulations previously mentioned. In Section 3, I will engage objections from cognitive science that attempt to show that religious knowledge is impossible, even from a proper functionalist perspective. Finally, I will then utilize the work that has been developed in this Element to develop an epistemic argument for God's existence. In doing this, I will attempt to bridge the gap between epistemology and natural theology.

1.2 Classical Foundationalism

When one asks a subject, S, why she believes that P, S will offer a reason, r1, which she thinks justifies her belief that P. Of course, one could continue to

---

[1] I am not alone in thinking this. See also Andrew Moon, "Recent Work in Reformed Epistemology," *Philosophy Compass*, 2016: https://doi.org/10.1111/phc3.12361.

ask S why she believes r1, and S might feel compelled to give another reason, say r2. This questioning will need to either end with a final reason, assume a reason that was already given, or S could continue to give reasons *ad infinitum*. This trilemma is known as Agrippa's Trilemma (Wright, 2013, p. 1114).

In Western analytic epistemology, the mainstream response to Agrippa's Trilemma is to endorse the final reason option. This is the position of the foundationalists. Foundationalism is the view that our noetic structure can be systematically bifurcated into basic beliefs and based beliefs. Basic beliefs are a subject's foundational beliefs; they are the beliefs on which the rest of our beliefs are based. The idea is that properly basic beliefs are such that they are held rationally apart from argumentation.

But not all basic beliefs can be considered properly basic. Classical foundationalists argue that basic beliefs are the beliefs that are incorrigible.

DePoe succinctly describes what is meant by incorrigibility:

> To say that a belief is incorrigible means that the subject stands in an uncorrectable position with respect to the truth of that belief. For instance, if someone is having an excruciating headache, nobody (not even a neuroscientist who has run a series of diagnostic tests on this person) is in a better epistemic position to correct this person and inform him that he is not experiencing a headache. Perhaps the simplest and most readily available form of incorrigible belief takes place when the subject is pointing to the qualities of his own experience in believing, "I am being appeared to *thusly.*" Incorrigible beliefs are impervious to falsehood, which guarantees a connection to truth at the most basic level of belief in classical foundationalism (DePoe, forthcoming).

Classical foundationalists are epistemic internalists. Roughly, epistemic internalists endorse that there is a required access condition that a subject needs to meet in order for her belief to be considered justified. This is contrasted with epistemic externalist theories. Epistemic externalism is roughly just the denial of the internalist access thesis. Externalist theories endorse that there is something outside of a subject's access, such as a reliable cognitive faculty, that is responsible, at least in part, for the belief's justification.

It should now be very clear that this view is not compatible with the thesis of Reformed epistemology. Belief that God exists, for example, is simply not a good candidate for being considered an incorrigible belief. While people might have supreme confidence that God exists, few people, I think, would be willing to say that it's impossible to be wrong about God's existence. Rather, instead of appealing to the possibility that religious belief can be properly basic, classical foundationalists, who are also theists, advance technical arguments for God's existence. So, it is not that knowledge of God is impossible, but rather, if humans are to possess knowledge that God exists, it will come from the success of arguments.

However, few people are classical foundationalists anymore. So, there might not be any good reason to accept the strenuous view that in order for S to know that God exists, S must have access to sufficiently good arguments that support God's existence. I now turn my attention to advancing four Plantingian responses to classical foundationalism.

1.3 Classical Foundationalism Rejected

First, Plantinga argues that classical foundationalism is self-referentially incoherent (Plantinga, 2000, p. 94). As we have seen above, the thesis of classical foundationalism is that, in order for a belief to be justified it must be incorrigible, or it must be properly based on another belief that is incorrigible. Plantinga argues that, if this is so, belief that classical foundationalism is true must itself either be incorrigible or be based on a belief that is incorrigible. However, the belief that classical foundationalism is true does not appear to be incorrigible or based on a belief that is incorrigible. Classical foundationalism then is self-defeating, as it fails to meet its own criteria.

It is worth noting that DePoe argues that classical foundationalism is not necessarily self-defeating. In "In Defense of Classical Foundationalism: A Critical Evaluation of Plantinga's Argument that Classical Foundationalism is Self-Refuting," DePoe argues that Plantinga has not shown that there are no good arguments that support the thesis of classical foundationalism; rather, he merely asserts it (DePoe, 2013, p. 249). DePoe thinks that Plantinga should articulate different arguments for classical foundationalism and judge each argument independently (DePoe, 2013, p. 250).

What would such an argument look like? Elsewhere, DePoe argues that we should endorse classical foundationalism, as classic foundationalism is the only theory that can capture a tight connection to truth (given that the foundation of our knowledge rests upon incorrigible beliefs), and make it such that internal rationality is a requirement for a subject's belief to be justified (DePoe, forthcoming). DePoe tries to prove this last point by way of Laurence BonJour's Norman the Clairvoyant case. It goes as follows:

> Norman, under certain conditions which usually obtain, is a completely reliable clairvoyant with respect to certain kinds of subject matter. He possesses no evidence or reasons of any kind for or against the general possibility of such a cognitive power or for or against the thesis that he possesses it. One day Norman comes to believe that the President is in New

York City, though he has no evidence either for or against this belief. In fact, the belief is true and results from his clairvoyant power under circumstances in which it is completely reliable (BonJour, 1985, p. 41).

Here, while Norman has a reliable faculty, Norman still seems irrational in holding to his belief. Reliability is not sufficient for justification. Rationality, at least according to BonJour, demands that Norman possess evidence for his belief. So, while DePoe seems sympathetic to externalist theories being able to account for a belief having the right connection to truth, DePoe does not think that externalist theories will fare well in accounting for a subject being internally rational.

There have been, however, various responses to BonJour's clairvoyant case. For example, Andrew Moon argues for an age of accountability principle, where any mature subject who utilizes an unknown faculty will need to have evidence of that faculty's reliability (Moon, 2018, p. 265). This is completely compatible with externalist theories. And given this is the case, I see no reason why the externalist could not employ this principle (or something like it) and be able to account for both the connection to truth and the internal rationality requirements that DePoe lays out. If that is the case, then we again have lost motivation for thinking that classical foundationalism is true. While we might not be able to say that it is self-defeating, it still seems right to say that minimally, it is not clear that there are good arguments for it. This suggests that classical foundationalism may still be vulnerable to self-defeat charges.

Second, Plantinga argues that, given classical foundationalism, most of our beliefs would not be justified. He points out that there are certain central beliefs that we all appear to hold, and yet there are no good arguments for them. Plantinga has in mind such beliefs as belief in other minds, belief in the uniformity of nature, and belief that the past was not created five minutes ago with the appearance of age. Since he holds it to be obvious that the beliefs in question are justified, he takes this to show that classical foundationalism must be false.

It is worth noting that attempts have been made to show that there are good arguments for the aforementioned beliefs (McGrew and McGrew, 2006), but such arguments have yet to convince most epistemologists. This, of course, does not show that the proposed arguments are bad; however, I think it is evidence that there is still a lot of work ahead for the classical foundationalist in addressing Plantinga's concerns.

Third, we should reject classical foundationalism because humans do not actually possess incorrigible beliefs. A belief being incorrigible is often glossed in truth-maker terminology. For example, it can be said that S cannot be wrong about her belief that P, given that she sees the relationship between the truth-maker and the truth-bearer. But we could be wrong about "seeing" the truth. What makes one think that they see the relationship between the truth-maker and truth-bearer is an experience or a certain phenomenology. This experience leads us to think that P is such that it could not be false. This experience, however, can be misleading. Plantinga makes this point when he states, "Before Russell showed him the error of his ways, Frege believed that for every property there is the set of just those things that display the property; and he believed that *a priori*. But he didn't see that it is true; it isn't true" (Plantinga, 1993, p. 106).

Finally, I'm not at all convinced that the requirements endorsed by classical foundationalists are actually necessary for a subject's belief to be justified. I have an intuition that justification, or even stronger epistemic states, such as warrant (to be defined at the end of the section), can be obtained without incorrigibility or sufficiently good arguments. However, in order to really make this case, I need to defend my preferred epistemology. Before I do this, I will first go through other contemporary epistemological theories that deviate significantly from classical foundationalism. First, I will engage two internalist epistemic theories,[2] and then I will engage two externalist epistemic theories. I will make clear that the following theories are compatible with the second tenet in Plantinga's religious epistemology, namely the tenet of Reformed epistemology. This will set up the next section, where I will argue for the tenet of proper functionalism.

1.4 Internalism: Phenomenal Conservatism

According to Martin Smith, phenomenal conservatism (PC) is a prominent view in epistemology that says "if it seems to one that P is true then, in the absence of defeaters, one has justification for believing that P is true." At the heart of this theory are seemings. Seemings are supposed to be a particular type of mental state that bears propositional content and a distinct sort of phenomenology (Smith, 2014, p. 141). Upon having a certain seeming(s), one is justified in making a natural doxastic response to affirm a belief related to that seeming.

If this is the case, then it is easy to imagine a scenario where it seems to S that God exists, and, in the absence of defeaters, S would be justified in believing that God exists. Logan Gage and Blake McAllister put this well:

> There are numerous people to whom it seems God exists when they are out in
> nature, when they pray, in their moments of joy and sorrow. Indeed, it is not
> uncommon for believers to undergo periods of time in which God's existence

---

[2] Epistemic disjunctivism is a hybrid theory of sorts. I categorize it below as an internalist theory given that it endorses an access condition. See Duncan Pritchard, *Epistemological Disjunctivism* (Oxford: Oxford University Press, 2012), 2–3.

appears woven into the very fabric of existence – they see his fingerprints everywhere. In these moments, God's existence can seem nearly as apparent as the existence of other human beings. The very idea of a world without God feels absurd. In accordance with PC, these theistic seemings provide non-inferential justification for believing that God exists. Defeaters (discussed more in the next section) can arise which remove this justification. But until they do, such believers appear well within their epistemic rights to believe that God exists, even if they are mistaken. (Gage and McAllister, forthcoming)

Gage and McAllister however, are inclined to think that when believers encounter sophisticated objections, they will need to deal with such objections by employing other types of evidence (Gage and McAllister, forthcoming). In this sense, the phenomenal conservative would be endorsing the thesis of Reformed epistemology, but also maintaining that arguments have an important role in the believer's doxastic process. Specifically, arguments are needed to continue to rationally affirm her religious convictions in light of attempted defeaters.

One concern that the phenomenal conservative often hears is that while a subject's seeming could show why she is within her right (i.e., justified) to believe the proposition in question, seemings are not tied to truth, and thus PC does not help us understand what is needed for a subject to possess knowledge. This is something that a phenomenal conservative will usually acknowledge (including Gage and McAllister). Something more is needed.

1.5 Epistemic Disjunctivism

Unlike PC, which is a theory of justification, epistemic disjunctivism (ED) is proposed as a paradigm epistemic theory of perceptual knowledge. That is to say, ED is proposed as an ideal case of perceptual knowledge; it is not an account of necessary and sufficient conditions. Roughly, the thesis of ED is that a perceptual belief constitutes knowledge if Subject S has reflective access to the property that confers justification, and the reason she has for believing that P, also entails that P is true (cf. Pritchard, 2012, p. 13).

Take the case of a subject believing that there is a tree in front of her as an example. S has paradigmatic knowledge that P if she has access to what rationally supports her belief, and what rationally supports her belief is factive. In this case, S's reason is a seeming that there is a tree in front of her. Since she has reflective access to this seeming and because, in this case, the seeming entails that there is a tree in front of her, S has paradigmatic knowledge. Kegan Shaw has recently proposed that we call seemings that entail the truth of S's belief *pneumings* (Shaw, 2016, p. 265). With that in mind, it is not hard to see how this can apply to religious belief.

God becomes present in the room with subject S. As a result, due to possessing a pneuming that God is present in the room, S believes that God is present in the room. S in this case would have paradigmatic knowledge. She has reflective access to this pneuming, and the pneuming entails the truth about God existing in the room.

There are questions, of course, about epistemic peer disagreement. How does S know that what she has access to is a pneuming and not a mere seeming? What should S do if S* believes -P and she also claims to have access to a pneuming? There are standard responses to these questions that the advocate of ED can utilize (Kelly, 2005. However, I'm not sure if her epistemological theory, in itself, can provide resources to handle these questions. As the reader will see in Sections 2 and 3, I think the theory that this Element will defend has better resources to address the questions of social epistemology. Moreover, and more importantly, this theory does not tell us what the jointly necessary and sufficient conditions are for justification or warrant. We need to look elsewhere for these. I now turn to engaging externalist theories of justification.

1.6 Reliabilism and Virtue Reliabilism

Probably the most well-known externalist account is reliabilism. For the purposes of this section, I will call the reliabilism that I have in mind *general reliabilism*. This will help distinguish it from virtue reliabilism, which will be addressed shortly after.

General reliabilism can be glossed in at least two different ways. First, it can be glossed to emphasize a reliable process such that it states, "S is justified in believing that P, iff S has a reliable process which is responsible for S believing that P." Second, it could also be glossed in such a way as to emphasize the evidence that S has, such that S's belief P is reliable insofar as S's evidence reliably leads S to produce P. It seems relatively easy to see how these theories are compatible with Reformed epistemology. Without too much controversy, one could make the following formulation for the first type of reliabilism:

> It is epistemically possible that S has a reliable faculty that produces in S the belief that God exists; and if such a faculty did produce the belief that God exists, S's belief that God exists would be justified.

With respect to the other type of general reliabilism, one could make the following formulation:

> S possesses evidence that God exists, and, if the evidence is such that it reliably
> leads S to the truth that God exists, S's belief that God exists is justified.

In the first case, the faculty could naturally produce the belief that God exists in the same way that it would naturally produce the belief that the universe is uniform or that there are other minds around us. The faculty could also produce the belief that God exists by way of utilizing an argument that supports the belief. In the second case, S could utilize seemings or arguments for God's existence to reliably get her to the truth that God exists. It seems clear that with respect to reliabilism, religious beliefs could be non-inferentially justified.

However, with reliabilism there is a concern that is known as the generality problem. Roughly, for process reliabilism, the problem is how to demarcate the token process that leads to reliability between those other processes that S might also possess, which are either not as reliable or not reliable at all. If we cannot demarcate what is actually doing the justifying, we fail to have a substantive theory. Feldman makes this point clear:

> For example, the process token leading to my current belief that it is sunny
> today is an instance of all the following types: the perceptual process, the
> visual process, processes that occur on Wednesday, processes that lead to
> true beliefs, etc. Note that these process types are not equally reliable.
> Obviously, then, one of these types must be the one whose reliability is
> relevant to the assessment of my belief. (Feldman, 1985, pp. 159–60)

There is another type of reliabilism that attempts to get around the generality problem. The relevant reliable processes are cognitive virtues. According to Sosa, "One has an intellectual virtue or faculty relative to an environment E if and only if one has an inner nature I in virtue of which one would mostly attain the truth and avoid error in a certain field of propositions F, when in certain conditions C" (Sosa, 1991, p. 284). The idea is that cognitive virtues include inductive, deductive, perceptual, and memory faculties.[3] Again, religious beliefs can easily be non-inferentially justified on this model.

> It is epistemically possible that S has a cognitive virtue 'm' that produces in S
> the belief that God exists; and if this was the case, S's belief that God exists
> would be justified.

It seems like what was repeated for general reliabilism can also be said for virtue reliabilism. The fact of the matter is that on these externalist accounts,

---

[3] Jason Baehr, Virtue Epistemology, *Internet Encyclopedia of Philosophy*, www.iep.utm
.edu/virtueep/.

religious belief can be justified, even apart from argument. There is another question, however, and that is a question about warrant. Take warrant to be the ingredient that separates mere true belief from knowledge. The idea is more closely related to S knowing that P, than S being within her epistemic right to believe that P. If epistemologists care about whether a subject can know that a proposition is true, she will need to give an account of warrant. But what is the correct view of warrant? Perhaps, one is inclined to think that justification equals warrant. On this view, the questions about justification and warrant are one in the same. However, if justification is roughly understood deontologically, I think something much stronger is needed for warrant. I do not take it, for example, that merely having a seeming or a cognitive virtue will be sufficient for warrant. I now turn to arguing for a proper functionalist theory of warrant.

2 The Plausibility of Proper Functionalism and Reformed Epistemology

2.1 Proper Functionalism

In order to demonstrate the plausibility of Plantinga's theory of warrant, I will first need to articulate it. After doing this, I will argue for each condition of his theory and explain why each condition is necessary for warrant. Having established as much, I will describe how beliefs, which historically have been targeted by skepticism, can be warranted once the proper function conditions are in place. This will help show the sufficient nature of Plantinga's theory and set up how Plantinga applies his theory to religious belief. Finally, after I articulate Plantinga's religious epistemology, I will briefly engage two objections to Plantinga's religious epistemology.

Plantinga's theory of warrant is as follows:

S's belief that P is warranted iff at the time S forms the belief that P,

(1) S's cognitive faculties are functioning properly,
(2) S's cognitive environment is sufficiently similar to the one for which S's cognitive faculties are designed,
(3) The design plan that governs the production of beliefs is aimed at producing true belief, and
(4) The design plan is a good one such that there is a high statistical (or objective) probability that a belief produced under these conditions will be true.[4]

---

[4] This is a paraphrase from Joseph Kim, *Reformed Epistemology and the Problem of Religious Diversity: Proper Function, Epistemic Disagreement, and Christian Exclusivism* (Eugene, OR: Pickwick Publications, 2011), 19. I chose Kim's layout of Plantinga's theory over Plantinga's own,

I will refer to (1) as the proper function condition, (2) as the epistemic environment condition, and (3) and (4) together as the truth-aimed condition. Presently, I will argue that condition (1) is a necessary condition for warrant. In order to argue for (1), I will first articulate Ernest Sosa's Swampman counterexample that is directed toward Plantinga's theory of warrant. I will then argue, contra Sosa, that the Swampman counterexample actually gives us good reason to affirm that proper function is a necessary condition for warrant. This is because without proper function, Swampman's beliefs should be seen as too lucky to constitute knowledge.

2.2 Sosa's Swampman and Swampman's Luck

Ernest Sosa develops his Swampman counterexample by first quoting Donald Davidson:

> Suppose lightning strikes a dead tree in a swamp; I am standing nearby. My body is reduced to its elements, while entirely by coincidence (and out of different molecules) the tree is turned into my physical replica. My replica, The Swampman, moves exactly as I did; according to its nature it departs the swamp, encounters and seems to recognize my friends, and appears to return their greetings in English. It moves into my houses and seems to write articles on radical interpretation. No one can tell the difference. But there *is* a difference. (Sosa, 1996, pp. 258–259; cf. Davidson, 1987)

Swampman was not created by God, nor did he come about through the process of millions of years of natural selection. Therefore, Swampman lacks a design plan.[5] And yet, if Swampman is going around doing basic addition or teaching children basic history, Sosa's intuition is such that Swampman still possesses knowledge. If Swampman possesses knowledge without proper function, then we would have a genuine counterexample to proper functionalism. I now turn to two responses to this counterexample.

2.3 Cognitive Science Takes on Swampman

Following Kenneth Boyce and Alvin Plantinga's (Boyce and Plantinga, 2012) lead, I argue elsewhere (McNabb, 2015) that the Swampman scenario actually

---

as Kim's layout is in schematic form. For the way Plantinga originally laid out his theory, see Alvin Plantinga, *Warrant and Proper Function* (New York: Oxford University Press, 1993), 46.

[5] Perhaps one thinks that one can advocate for an Aristotelian/Thomistic conception of human nature and endorse that Swampman can come about from these random conditions with cognitive faculties that have design plans. This of course would avoid the problem for the proper functionalist altogether. It would not be such that Swampman is a counterexample to proper function at all. A person who advocates for this view should in fact endorse that in order for a subject to know that P, the subject's faculties need to achieve their ends. For evidence that Thomas Aquinas affirmed this view, see Eleanore Stump, "Aquinas on the Foundations of Knowledge," *Canadian Journal of Philosophy 21 Supplement Volume 17* (1991): 148–9.

supports the proper functionalist thesis. Since Gettier (1963)[6] it is understood that a proposed theory of warrant should be incompatible with the belief in the question being true, warranted, and relevantly lucky. There are of course different ways a belief can be lucky, and there is a question as to which cases of luck are relevant as it pertains to a subject possessing knowledge. What I will be arguing is that Swampman's beliefs do not constitute knowledge, given that his beliefs suffer from what I call cognitive luck.

A subject's belief suffers from cognitive luck if it is extremely serendipitous that a cognitive faculty produces a true belief. Take, for example, an individual who, due to cognitive malfunction, believes that all objects are red. Surely it could be said that this individual would have lots of true beliefs if she attended a communist decor party. It is completely serendipitous that her cognitive faculties are producing true beliefs, however. Her beliefs clearly do not constitute knowledge.

Swampman is a paradigm case of an individual whose beliefs suffer from cognitive luck. His faculties have no way in which they should operate. It is not as if they should produce the belief that $2 + 2 = 4$ or the belief that in 2017, Neil Gorsuch was confirmed as a Justice of the United States Supreme Court. Nonetheless, his faculties just so happen to produce these beliefs. This seems extremely serendipitous.

Swampman can be contrasted with Davidson. When Davidson forms the belief that $2 + 2 = 4$ or that Gorsuch is a member of the Supreme Court, Davidson's faculties are operating in the manner in which they ought to operate. The only difference between Davidson and Swampman is that Davidson's faculties have a design plan. It seems as if proper function (and the conditions related to proper function) is what is needed to prevent cases of cognitive luck.

There is another reason to think that the Swampman scenario provides plausibility to the proper function condition. Kenneth Boyce and Andrew Moon (2016) argue that the central intuition (CI) behind why people initially think Swampman is a counterexample to proper functionalism can be captured as follows:

> (CI) If a belief B is warranted for a subject S and another subject S* comes to hold B in the same way that S came to hold B in a relevantly similar environment to the one in which S came to hold B, then B is warranted for S*. (Boyce and Moon, 2016, p. 2990)

Boyce and Moon argue against CI by way of presenting various cases. First, Boyce and Moon point out that according to cognitive science, young children

---

[6] I will expound on Gettier's work in Section 2.5.

produce the belief in object permanence. Boyce and Moon then move on to invite the reader to imagine the following scenarios:[7]

Case 1: Billy is a human infant who is an unknowing participant in an experimental program concerning early childhood cognitive development. In the
process of being experimented upon, he sees a red ball go behind a screen,
out of sight, and, via an unlearned doxastic response, forms the belief that the
round object he just saw is behind the screen. (Boyce and Moon, 2016,
p. 2997)

Boyce and Moon think that Case 1 should be seen as uncontroversial. Billy's faculties are working in the way in which they should. There is simply no reason to think that Billy's belief is not warranted.

Case 2: Billy sees a red ball go behind a screen. But due to a genetic birth
defect, he has an abnormal doxastic response to that input and forms the
belief that the round object he just saw has ceased to exist. (Boyce and Moon,
2016, p. 2997)

Similar to Case 1, Boyce and Moon think that the case should be seen as uncontroversial. It is evident that Billy lacks warrant. Billy's cognitive mal-function seems to make it such that, his belief, even if somehow true, is too fortuitous to be warranted.

Case 3: All goes as it did in Case 2. However, owing to the design of the
cognitive experiments to which Billy is being subjected, red objects that
pass behind the screen placed in front of Billy are (as soon as they are
behind the screen and out of Billy's sight) instantly annihilated by a powerful laser (which is also behind the screen and out of Billy's sight). We'll
also add that Billy only tends to have the sort of abnormal doxastic
response described in Case 2 when he sees *red* objects being occluded. In
other cases when he sees objects of different colors occluded, he believes in
their continued existence just as any other human child would. (Boyce and
Moon, 2016, p. 2997)

The only difference between Cases 2 and 3 is that there are agents who, unbeknownst to Billy, are intentionally destroying the red objects with a laser. Again, Boyce and Moon think that Billy's belief is not warranted in this case.

---

[7] In part, the following summaries of Boyce and Moon's scenarios have also been informed by Jeff
Tolly, 'Swampman: A Dilemma for Proper Functionalists,' forthcoming in *Synthese*.

Case 4: Zork, unlike Billy, is an alien child who lives on another planet, although members of his species are very human-like (so human-like, in fact, that even down to the molecular level, it is difficult to distinguish them from human beings). Furthermore, Zork's planet is very much like Earth, with one important exception. Owing to some odd features of its magnetic field and some currently unknown (to Earth scientists) quantum phenomenon, strange, macroscopic-sized, red, spherical particles frequently pop into existence in the presence of observers on Zork's planet and then disappear. These particles have a further odd property. If one of them pops into existence in the presence of a group of observers, then if any one of those observers stops observing that particle, it immediately ceases to exist. Zork (who is also an unknowing subject of cognitive experiments on early child-hood development being conducted by adult members of his species) sees one of these particles go behind a screen and via an unlearned doxastic response, forms the belief that the round object he just saw has ceased to exist. (Boyce and Moon, 2016, pp. 2997–8)

Boyce and Moon think that Zork's belief clearly has warrant. Zork's faculties are designed to produce the belief that red objects disappear when they are not observed, and Zork is in the right epistemic environment for which his faculties are designed.

Case 5: Billy has been abducted by aliens of Zork's species and taken to Zork's planet. Furthermore, Billy has exactly the same sorts of belief-forming tendencies that he was stipulated to have in Case 3. Billy sees one of the strange, red, spherical particles from Zork's world pass behind a screen and believes that it has ceased to exist. (Boyce and Moon, 2016, p. 2998)

Even though Billy is in an environment that is congenial to his belief-forming processes, there still seems something serendipitous about Billy's belief. His belief still seems to lack warrant, regardless of the change in environment.

Case 6: Billy and Zork are both present in a laboratory on Zork's planet. Both simultaneously observe one of the strange, red, spherical particles from Zork's planet pass behind a screen. All goes for Zork as it did in Case 4 and all goes for Billy as it did in Case 5. Consequently, both Zork and Billy form the belief that the round object that they just saw has ceased to exist. (Boyce and Moon, 2016)

Both of the young children produce the belief that red objects disappear when they go unobserved. And, given the physics of the planet, the red objects actually do disappear. And yet it seems that when Billy forms the belief that the red object disappears, his belief lacks warrant, while Zork's belief would possess warrant. Why is that? Boyce and Moon argue that the best way to explain this situation is that Billy's faculties lack proper function and Zork's faculties do not.

2.4 The Return of Swampman

Jeff Tolly has recently argued against the conclusion of Boyce and Moon's argument (Tolly, forthcoming). Tolly thinks that Case 3 is too ambiguous. He argues that one could interpret it in one of the following ways:

Case 3a: The scientists at Billy's experimental facility are committed to locking Billy in the facility for his entire life. Through elaborate locking mechanisms and deception, he will never get out. Their goal is to destroy every red ball that becomes obscured to Billy throughout his entire life.

Case 3b: In one week's time, the scientists at Billy's facility will let Billy go free in the outside world, where he will proceed to make all sorts of incorrect *non-existence* ascriptions to every single red ball that he sees passing behind an obstruction. (Tolly, forthcoming, p. 7)

In case 3b, Tolly agrees with Boyce and Moon in that Billy's belief would lack warrant. However, it is not clear to him that this is the case for 3a. In order to avoid a belief being too lucky, Tolly thinks that a belief needs to meet the Content Based Reliability Condition (CBR).

> (CBR) Necessarily, where S's token process t involves forming a belief that p on the (complete) basis of mental states m, t confers warrant only if the type T, [forming beliefs in propositions sufficiently similar to p on the basis of mental states sufficiently similar to m] has a high reliability measurement across a reference class of all possible belief-forming events sufficiently close to t in which S undergoes T processes. (Tolly, forthcoming, p. 8)

In case 3a, Billy's token type process is modally reliable across nearby belief-forming events, so according to CBR, one should think that Billy's belief is warranted. Aware that this still might not be clear to some, Tolly gives cases 7 and 8 in hopes of making a convincing case that in 3a, Billy's belief would be warranted.

Case 7: Zork is born with a cognitive abnormality for his species that gives him a disposition to think that red spheres (just like any colored sphere) continue existing even when they become obscured. He forms these sorts of judgments "in the same way" any normal human would. Interestingly enough, unbeknownst to any other member of his species, a year before Zork was born, a solar storm blew through their atmosphere and changed the planet's magnetic field properties. Now, red spheres *don't disappear* when no one's looking – however, everyone on the planet (except for Zork) still mistakenly thinks that they go out of existence. Zork is rather introverted and keeps to himself, choosing to live far away from other members of his species. He never realizes (and lacks any disposition to realize) that the rest of his species radically disagrees with him about the persistence of obscured red spheres. (Tolly, forthcoming, p. 13)

Case 8: Zork has the same cognitive abnormality as Case 7, but the solar storm never blew through. In addition, Zork was born into a large but closed-off facility on his planet. Unbeknownst to everyone, including Zork, the radioactive material in the walls of this facility counter-acts the planet's odd quantum-phenomenon, so that *inside* the facility, red spheres behave just like any other colored object: they remain in existence when obscured. Zork lives out his days in this facility. In fact, he has no idea that there's even an outside world, and he also has no way to get out. (Tolly, forthcoming, p. 13)

Tolly contends that Cases 8 and 3 are analogous such that, if Zork has warrant in Case 8, then Billy has warrant in Case 3.

> Upon reflection, Zork seems to have warrant in Case 8 just like Case 7. Here, the main difference between these cases is that there are some *spatially* nearby possible belief-forming events in which Zork misjudges persistence. But these possibilities are *modally* far away, and as I suggest above, it's modal distance that determines warrant-enabling reliability. I contend that Case 8 and Case 3a are analogous in the following sense: if Zork has warrant in Case 8, then so does Billy in Case 3a. Of course, the subject in 3a denies the persistence of some object while the subject in Case 8 ascribes persistence. But this difference doesn't seem like it could ground a difference in warrant. (Tolly, forthcoming).

So, is the fact that the token process in question is reliable across nearby belief-forming events what makes it such that Billy's belief should no longer seem sufficiently lucky? I'm dubious of this claim. In Case 8, Zork's beliefs about red objects still seem too lucky to constitute knowledge, not only for reasons mentioned in my first response to the Swampman objection, but also because there is still something incredibly lucky about producing a belief by way of cognitive malfunction; and yet, by way of being in a fortuitous situation, Zork's environment is such that the belief produced is true.

Perhaps Tolly is subconsciously assuming that the token faculty somehow has a connection to the environment such that the connection explains why the belief is produced. But there is not any sort of relation. The following scenario, I think, can make my point clearer:

Case 9: Billy was born with a cognitive malfunction. The cognitive malfunction produced in Billy the belief that objects possess conscious souls. By mere coincidence, Billy was born in an evil wizard's lair where, in fact, the wizard inserted conscious souls into the objects in the lair. There was a curse in the lair that never allowed Billy to leave. Billy spent all of his life alone in the lair.

I am not aware of any significant difference between Case 9 and Case 8. And yet, if Billy in Case 9 lacks warrant, then it seems to me that Zork should lack warrant in Cases 7 and 8. And with that, Tolly's response does not undermine Boyce and Moon's argument. The fact that Billy in Case 3 meets the CBR requirement does not somehow guarantee that a subject's belief will not possess cognitive luck. Billy does not know. Thus, while I think Tolly's objection is interesting, I think Boyce and Moon's point stands. The Billy and Zork scenario is positive evidence for the proper functionalist thesis.

2.5 Epistemic Environment Condition

Having now established (1) of Plantinga's theory, I will move on to demonstrating the plausibility of (2). In order to demonstrate that one could have proper function and yet not have warrant due to the lack of a right epistemic environment, it will be important to discuss the Gettier cases. The possibility of Gettier scenarios will be my main argument for (2). After I establish how Gettier helps demonstrate the necessity of (2) for warrant, I will move on to demonstrating both (3) and (4) collectively.

In the early 1960s Edmund Gettier (Gettier, 1963) published a three-page paper demonstrating how the classical tripartite analysis of knowledge failed in certain counterexamples. One of the examples that Gettier used was that of Smith and Jones. Smith and Jones have applied for a job, and Smith has strong evidence for the belief d: "Jones is the man who will get the job, and Jones has 10 coins in his pocket." Proposition d entails e: "The man who will get the job has ten coins in his pocket." But, little did Smith know, Jones would not be getting the job; however, the man who would get the job has 10 coins in his pocket – namely himself. Thus, even though d is false, e, which is entailed by d, is true. Though Smith is justified in his assertion of e, and e is true, it would be far-reaching to say Smith knew e. Thus, the traditional view of true, justified belief as knowledge is lacking.

More counterexamples like those espoused in Gettier's original paper have proliferated. All of these counterexamples to the traditional view of knowledge have been dubbed Gettier cases. One of the most famous examples of these can be seen in Carl Ginet's Wisconsinites example (Goldman, 1992, p. 102).[8]

In this example, a man named Henry is driving in the countryside of Wisconsin. Henry would generally expect to see barns, cows, tractors, and other things that are associated with this type of environment. However, unlike the normal environment to which Henry is accustomed, he unknowingly finds himself in a town where certain Wisconsinites have erected dozens of barn facades alongside a real barn. Moreover, Henry just happens to go near a real barn in the midst of the dozens of fake barns, and he forms the belief that there is a barn in front of him. Henry appears to be justified in believing it is a barn, and, indeed, it is a barn; however, in virtue of all the fake barns around it, one would be hard-pressed to say this judgement constitutes actual knowledge.

Keith Lehrer proposes another counterexample to the tripartite view of knowledge. In this example, Smith has a Ford but, unbeknownst to him, a meteorite shower occurs and destroys his car; however, he had previously entered in a raffle to win a car and again, unbeknownst to him, he has simultaneously won a Ford. Thus, Smith has true and justified belief about having a Ford – but, again, he would lack knowledge that he has one (Lehrer, 1965).

How do these Gettier examples demonstrate that proper function is not a sufficient condition for warrant? In regard to the case of the barn facades, one could postulate that there is an individual who has properly functioning faculties and those faculties produce the true belief that a barn is in front of them. But because the individual could have just as easily walked in any other direction and then would have run into a barn façade, it is only by chance that this belief is true. Since the proper function condition is in place, it follows one could have proper function and yet not have warrant. Thus, there needs to be something added to the proper function condition.

Similarly, in the Smith has a Ford case, one could postulate that Smith's faculties are functioning appropriately. Smith is not experiencing any cognitive malfunction and he appears to be acting epistemically responsibly in accordance with his cognitive design plan. However, Smith lacks warrant for his belief that he owns a Ford. An environment where your Ford is destroyed by a random meteorite and yet you simultaneously win a Ford from a contest is not the type of environment in which your faculties are meant to operate. As with the barn façade example, the particular environment that one is in can bring about accidental true beliefs. What these Gettier examples demonstrate is that

---

[8] Alvin Goldman credits the example to Carl Ginet in Alvin Goldman, *Philosophy Meets the Cognitive and Social Sciences* (Cambridge, MA: MIT Press, 1992), 102.

the environment in which one's cognitive faculties operate needs to be one for which they have been designed.[9]

The epistemic environment condition should be seen as guaranteeing safety. Roughly speaking, it is a condition that prevents true belief from counting as knowledge if it would have been believed and yet been false in a close possible world. All of this being so, I think (2) seems to be a plausible condition. I will now move on to arguing for the plausibility of (3) and (4).

2.6 The Truth-Aimed Condition

In addition to having cognitive faculties that are functioning properly and being in an environment for which the faculties were designed, Plantinga argues that the design plan would need to be one that is aimed at producing true beliefs. Moreover, it would need to be a good one in that there is a high statistical probability that the belief or beliefs produced under these conditions would be true.

In regard to (3), take the example of a malevolent deity who out of boredom creates human beings whose design plan is to produce all sorts of crazy beliefs. In addition to this, the malevolent deity creates an environment that will encourage their design plan to produce all sorts of crazy beliefs.[10] If we granted that the discussed conditions of warrant were in place when an unfortunate soul produced the crazy belief that he was created by a malevolent deity to produce crazy beliefs, would this be enough for the unfortunate soul to be warranted? This is unlikely, as there is still something serendipitous about his belief, which is due primarily to the design plan not being aimed toward truth.

Finally, in regard to (4), not only would there be a need for a design plan that is aimed at producing true beliefs, but also one that has a high probability of producing true beliefs.[11] It is possible that we were created by an incompetent designer, and though he had good intentions and aimed man's

---

[9] Plantinga distinguishes between maxi and mini environments. A maxi environment is the global environment that we find ourselves in. That is, it is an environment where we would expect to see middle-sized objects and the like. As Boyce puts it, a mini environment is "a much more specific state of affairs, one that includes, for a given exercise of one's cognitive faculties E resulting in a belief B, all of the epistemically relevant circumstances obtaining when B is formed (though diminished with respect to whether B is true)." See, Kenneth Boyce, "Proper Functionalism," *Internet Encyclopedia of Philosophy*, www.iep.utm.edu/prop-fun/. The Gettier examples articulated above would specifically be addressing the need for a mini environment. We need not emphasize the specifics for the purposes of this work, however. We can simply talk about needing the right environment.

[10] See Michael Bergmann, *Justification without Awareness* (New York: Oxford University Press, 2006), 135

[11] See Michael Bergmann, *Justification without Awareness* (New York: Oxford University Press, 2006), 135

faculties towards producing true beliefs, the poor design of those faculties would lead to man's faculties rarely achieving the intended goal of arriving at true beliefs. It is not enough to have a faculty achieve its goal every once in a while. Rather, the design plan must consistently yield true beliefs. If it only succeeded every one hundred tries, it would make any true belief produced somewhat of an accident. This would, again, strip away the possibility for a subject to obtain warrant and thus establishes the necessity of (4) for warrant.

In addition to arguing that his conditions are necessary for warrant, Plantinga also argues for his theory by way of showing how successful his theory is when it is applied to beliefs that have traditionally been targeted by skeptical arguments. His goal is to show that his theory of warrant has the explanatory scope as well as the explanatory power to explain how the beliefs targeted by skepticism could be warranted. If Plantinga's theory of warrant can solve the problem of skepticism and show how such beliefs are warranted more convincingly than the alternatives available, this would at least suggest that his theory is plausibly true.

Even though Plantinga interacts with beliefs about memory, the reality of the past, other minds, testimony, perception, and the uniformity of nature, my aim in this overview is simply to explain how he answers the problem of skepticism about beliefs that are obtained by means of perception and testimony. Applying Plantinga's theory of warrant to the aforementioned beliefs will also help provide evidence that the conditions mentioned are sufficient for warrant.

2.7 Perception

Can we obtain knowledge from perception? Plantinga argues that we can, and he does this by applying his theory of warrant. He argues that we normally come to our perceptual beliefs in a "basic" way, that is, in a way that does not depend on other beliefs (Plantinga, 1993, p. 93). When we perceive that a squirrel is running in our backyard, we have a particular phenomenology, and it is in virtue of this that we form (or at least partly form) the belief that a squirrel just ran through the backyard. This belief does not come about through reflecting on certain propositions, or through having infallible beliefs; rather, perceptual beliefs are naturally produced by our cognitive faculties without requiring the mediation of propositions.[12]

Holding this account of perceptual belief formation to be broadly correct, Plantinga develops the following key argument: If one's faculties are

---

[12] I am aware that in contemporary cognitive science literature there exists a preference to use the term "cognitive systems" instead of "cognitive faculties." Nonetheless, due to the abundance of proper functionalist literature that already uses the phrase "cognitive faculties" it is prudent for me to continue in this tradition, given the main focus of the thesis.

functioning properly in the environment for which they are meant, and they have a design plan that is aimed toward producing true beliefs, and there is a high statistical probability that beliefs produced from the design plan will be true, then perceptual beliefs formed under these conditions will be warranted (Plantinga, 1993, p. 89). Plantinga does not hold that a subject has to believe or know that these conditions are in place in order to have a warranted belief; rather, as long as these conditions are in place, the subject's belief will be warranted.

Plantinga briefly entertains the possibility that one could come to hold a particular perceptual belief by cumulative means that would include inductive methods and testimony. He gives the example of a child who, upon experiencing something treely, finds out from his mother that what he perceives is called a tree. He later finds a papier-mâché model that resembles a tree, and he goes on to form, by induction, the belief that he perceives a tree. However, he then finds out through testimony that trees are not made out of papier-mâché. He thus finely tunes his belief in what a tree is so that the next time he experiences either a tree or a papier-mâché model, he identifies it correctly. Plantinga is willing to grant all of this provided it is accepted that there is some component of perceptual belief that is basic, in the sense that he has defined, and that could only be warranted given an account of proper function along the lines that he suggests (Plantinga, 1993, p. 101).

2.8 Testimony

In *Warrant and Proper Function*, Plantinga starts his section on testimony by quoting a famous passage from Thomas Reid. Reid states, "[T]he wise author of nature hath planted in the human mind a propensity to rely on human testimony before we can give a reason for doing so" (Plantinga, 1993, p. 77; cf. Reid, 1983, pp. 281–282). Plantinga clarifies what Reid means by arguing that beliefs based on testimony are not formed by way of a clever inductive or abductive argument; rather, we obtain them through a special mechanism. This is important because, if it can be established, one would have to make room in one's epistemological system for the method by which beliefs based on testimony could be warranted apart from argumentation. This would be the case for most of our beliefs that are based upon testimony; this includes beliefs about scientific theories, past results of scientific experiments, beliefs about things that happened in history, geographical locations, people's names (including your own name), and so on (Plantinga, 1993, p. 77).

One might be tempted to argue that when we accept testimony, we do so because we have a reason to accept the reliability of the testimony-giver (that is the testifier). Perhaps we use our memory to think about all of the times this testimony-giver was right, or maybe we think about the reliability of other testimony-givers who at one time were in analogous circumstances to the current testimony-giver. After doing this, we might decide if we are justified in accepting the current testimony. Plantinga argues that this is not typically how we acquire beliefs by way of testimony, though he acknowledges that we do come to some beliefs in this manner.

In order to bring one's intuition to concede this point, Plantinga deploys the example of a five-year-old whose dad tells him that Australia is a large country and it occupies an entire continent by itself. The five-year-old does not think (normally) of past times when his dad has been reliable; rather, he seems to have a natural inclination to believe his dad. Plantinga uses this example as evidence that our cognitive faculties are inclined to accept the testimony of others as soon as we develop a certain cognitive ability. This inclination to accept testimony as a source of potential knowledge seems to be a natural part of our cognitive design plan, and it is present when our faculties are functioning properly (Plantinga, 1993, p. 80).

There are two more relevant ideas that Plantinga elaborates on in his section on testimony. First, just because we have a natural inclination to accept testimony as a potential source of knowledge, it does not follow that we cannot learn to discipline this inclination in light of certain experiences. Plantinga notes that we learn not to accept the testimony of politicians who want our vote. We also discipline our inclination to accept what we hear when we are listening to a dispute and we refrain from making a decision until we have heard both sides (Plantinga, 1993, p. 80).

Second, in order to produce a warranted belief, it seems likely that the design plan is such that the belief in question must come about through a warranted testimony cycle. For example, if someone intentionally lies to me and tells me that Santa Claus exists, even if it happened to be true (he does exist!) I would not be warranted in believing that he exists. This will also save us from possible Gettier scenarios, where you have a true belief that is justified, but it lacks warrant because it is based on faulty premises (Plantinga, 1993, p. 83).

2.9 Plantigian Religious Epistemology

Plantinga does not attempt to use his theory of warrant to prove that God exists; rather, he aims to show that his religious epistemology is epistemically possible, in other words, that it is consistent with what we know (Plantinga, 2000, p. 168). He argues that, if God exists, and if He has successfully constituted subject S's cognitive faculties in such a way that, when they are properly functioning in the environment for which they are meant, they would produce the belief that God exists, then S's belief that God exists could be warranted even apart from argumentation. Since belief in the existence of God would not depend on arguments and would be formed through the proper function of S's cognitive faculties, S's belief should be considered properly basic (Plantinga, 2000, p. 168). He calls his model of warranted religious belief the Aquinas/Calvin model (AC model).[13] And, like Calvin before him, he calls the cognitive process that enables awareness of God the *sensus divinitatis* (Plantinga, 2000, pp. 170–172).

Plantinga attempts to explain why some people fail to form the belief that God exists[14] by arguing that, if the Christian story is true, then something like sin has come into the world and has damaged our belief-forming structure. Thus, while God intended that we would always perceive Him, sin has weakened (though not destroyed) our awareness to the extent that sometimes it does not function at all (Plantinga, 2000, p. 213).

Plantinga extends his discussion of how belief in the existence of God could be warranted to cover the much more specific case of belief in Christianity;[15] arguing that, if Christianity were true, it would likely be warranted. He does this by further articulating his extended Aquinas/Calvin model (EAC model). On this model, Holy Scripture, which has both a primary author (the Holy Spirit) and numerous secondary authors (the human writers), acts as a testimony to S in that it conveys the truth of the Gospel message. The Spirit of God then

---

[13] Plantinga calls this the Aquinas/Calvin model because he believes Aquinas and Calvin articulated something very similar in their respective works. For Thomas Aquinas, see *Summa Theologia* I, q. 2, a. 1, ad 1. For Calvin, see John Calvin, *Institutes of the Christian Religion*, tr. Ford Lewis Battles and ed. John T. McNeill (Philadelphia: Westminster Press, 1960), 44.

[14] It seems to me that Plantinga's epistemology is completely compatible with the fact and actually predicts that people will have very different views about God. All sorts of different articulations of the transcendent are to be expected, given that sin has damaged the faculty that produces belief that God exists.

[15] For Plantinga, the Gospel message is the essence of the Christian religion. Thus, if belief in the Gospel message were warranted, belief in Christianity would be warranted. By Gospel message Plantinga has in mind something like the following story: God created the cosmos and all things in it. God, specifically, had in mind bringing about human life in His image, and so He created man with free will. Instead of loving God with all of his heart, mind, and strength, man served his own needs and broke off communion with God. As a response to this, in the way of the ultimate love story, God the Son became man, born of a virgin, in order to love God the Father in the way man should have loved Him. He loved His Father to the point of suffering the consequences of the world's sins on a cross and He died. This, then, pleased God the Father, as by the Holy Spirit He raised His Son from the dead, three days later. In doing this, God justified and vindicated His Son and is in the current process of reconciling all of the cosmos back into communion with Himself.

instigates (I take it that this can be seen as a form of giving a testimony) S to see that the Gospel message is true (Plantinga, 2000, p. 252). The testimony about the Gospel message can be accepted by S, in part, because the Spirit would improve on or repair any cognitive damage (damage that was the result of sin) that S would have. The result of this cognitive restoration would be S's faith that the Gospel message is true. Plantinga argues, if the EAC model were correct and God really was testifying by His Spirit to S that the Gospel message is true, and if S found herself believing that the Gospel message is true, then S's belief that the Gospel message is true could be warranted (Plantinga, 2000, p. 285).

2.10 Are Religious Beliefs Really Properly Basic?

Michael Tooley argues that since there is no reliable religious belief-forming faculty, religious beliefs are not properly basic (Plantinga and Tooley, 2008, p. 243). For Tooley, properly basic beliefs are beliefs that have attracted massive intersubjective agreement. He states:

> Consider the cases where there are reliable belief-forming mechanisms – as with perception, memory, and deductive reasoning. What one finds in those cases is that there is a massive intersubjective agreement. Two observers, who are near one another and looking in roughly the same direction, will offer descriptions of what they see that agree to a striking extent, and with an enormous amount of detail. (Plantinga and Tooley, 2008)

Since religious beliefs elicit a great amount of epistemic disagreement among peers, it would not appear that they are produced from a reliable belief-forming faculty. How would Plantinga respond to Tooley's claims? The answer may be found in his explanation of why there is such religious diversity to begin with (Plantinga and Tooley, 2008, p. 199). As mentioned earlier in this section, Plantinga argues that sin has damaged the religious belief-forming faculty and that it needs to be repaired by the Holy Spirit. This is not to say that sin has damaged the totality of our cognitive system in a significant way, or that our memory or perceptual faculties are not reliable; rather, there is damage to our religious belief-producing faculty.

If multiple individuals had damaged memory faculties and each individual experienced the same events for a week, it would be a safe assumption that there would be radical differences in each individual's recall of the previous week. It would not follow, however, that the disagreement between these individuals proves that there is no reliable memory faculty, or that the memory faculty should not ever be considered to be a reliable means to obtain knowledge; at best, it proves that there is a damaged faculty. And if Plantinga's story is right, there would be some whose faculties would be in the process of being repaired to full optimal function.

2.11 Is Religious Diversity a Problem for the Plantingian?

Does the mere fact that there is religious diversity create a problem for the Plantingian? We can summarize the objection from religious diversity as follows: Even if one were to grant that religious belief could be warranted without the subject of the belief having access to the internal properties that ground the warrant for that belief, it would appear that one would not be rational in holding to any particular religious doctrine because of the vast number of other conflicting religious beliefs available. This type of argument often utilizes equal weight theory (Kelly, 2005), which holds that one should give equal weight to both an epistemic peer's belief and to one's own. The argument can best be illustrated in the following syllogism:

(1) It is unreasonable to hold to one's views in the face of disagreement since one would need some positive reason to privilege one's views over one's opponent['s views].
(2) No such reason is available since the disagreeing parties are epistemic peers and have access to the same evidence.
(3) Therefore, one should give equal weight to the opinion of an epistemic peer and to one's own opinion in the case of epistemic disagreement (Kim, 2011, pp. 49–50).

The Plantigian Joseph Kim has argued that equal weight theory should not be seen as a threat to Christian belief for at least three reasons (Kim, 2011, pp. 46–65). First, one could accept equal weight theory but deny that followers of other religions are epistemic peers. If the Spirit of God actually repaired one subject's cognitive faculty and testified to that subject, then that subject would not be in the same epistemic situation as a subject who mistakenly perceives that God has revealed Himself (and a different religion) to them. The latter subject's belief could have been a product of wish fulfilment or some cognitive malfunction (Kim, 2011, p. 65). This disparity between the subjects would hold even if an onlooker could not tell the difference between the two.

Second, it would further appear that if equal weight theory were true, one could not have knowledge about the right conclusions to philosophical paradoxes and even common-sense philosophical beliefs (these would even include philosophical beliefs about knowledge of other minds). This is because there exist epistemic peers who differ on whether such beliefs could be justified or warranted (Kim, 2011, pp. 54–55). This thought can also be applied to science.

Take the example of quantum mechanics: If one top scientist takes a non-realist view about the interpretation of the wave function, while his epistemic peer takes a realist view, it would follow, according to the equal weight theory, that both of them would need to withhold belief about the correct interpretation.

Lastly, Kim sees good reason to reject equal weight theory as it would appear to be self-defeating (Kim, 2011, p. 61). If philosophers in one category, say category A, affirmed equal weight theory, while another category of philosophers, say category B, denied equal weight theory, it would follow that philosophers in neither category would be warranted in believing in equal weight theory. This is the case presuming only that they were all epistemic peers lacking any convincing reasons to privilege one belief over another. Kim believes that the reasons given here provide us enough justification to reject equal weight theory and with it this version of the problem of religious diversity altogether. Having now argued for Plantinga's religious epistemology, I will move on to entertaining objections from cognitive science that attempt to undermine Plantinga's religious epistemology. Since I take it that objections from cognitive science are the best ones against Plantinga's epistemology, I will dedicate a whole section to engaging them.

3 Cognitive Science of Religion and Debunking Arguments

3.1 Cognitive Science of Religion

A computational theory of mind (CTM) is roughly the thesis that the human mind is a computer. It is understood that CTM is the underlining theory behind cognitive science.[16] Cognitive science, roughly, is the interdisciplinary study of the mind that involves neuroscience, psychology, sociology, and philosophy (cf. Barrett, 2011, p. 5). Cognitive science of religion (CSR) is a subfield within cognitive science that attempts to study the human brain as a computer, with respect to religious belief. Currently, the paradigm view in CSR is that belief in God is an evolutionary spandrel. There are different models that attempt to explain how religious belief is an evolutionary spandrel. I now turn to discussing one such model.

3.2 HAAD and a Theory of Mind

The human mind naturally perceives the world through teleology. The mind projects teleology, even when it is not there. Deborah Kelemen calls this

---

[16] Marcin Milkowski, "The Computational Theory of Mind," *Internet Encyclopedia of Philosophy*, www.iep.utm.edu/compmind/.

phenomena *promiscuous teleology* (Kelemen, 1999). Kelemen is responsible for various studies that give significant credence to the view that the human mind naturally perceives teleology. In one study, Kelemen asked 7- to 8-year-olds various questions relating to animals and non-living objects. Famously, one of the questions asked was "Why are rocks pointy?" and children would respond with teleological explanations such as "so that animals wouldn't sit on them" (Kelemen 1999). Kelemen also studied adults and their preference for teleology. Educated adults and non-educated differed in their preference for teleological explanations. The former preferred naturalistic explanations (Kelemen and Rosset, 2009) while the latter preferred teleological explanations (Casler and Kelemen, 2008). However, it is worth mentioning that when the educated adults were asked to answer in a speedy manner, the preference for teleological explanations increased. It is also worth mentioning that these results are not just unique to those individuals living in one part of the Western world. The studies are consistent across cultures, including in Finland (Järnefelt et al., 2015; cf. Kundert and Edman, 2017, p. 86) and China (see Rottman et al., 2017; cf. Kundert and Edman, 2017, pp. 89–90).

Guthrie argues that natural selection has equipped humans with a better-safe-than-sorry mechanism, known more formally as a Hyper Agency Detection Device (HADD) (Guthrie, 1993; cf. Barrett, 2011, p. 100). That is, natural selection has shaped the human mind to be significantly sensitive to agency. Possessing a device that detects agency too much will likely lead an organism to survive, or at least more so than a device that does not detect agency enough.

Humans are not just equipped with a HADD, however; they also possess a faculty known as a Theory of Mind (ToM), which helps make sense of and understand other agents (Norenzayan, 2015, p. 15; Barrett, 2011, pp. 74–77). For example, it helps a teacher understand the intentions and beliefs of a student who raises her hand in class, and it helps a doctor understand the pain that a patient is going through. It is a faculty that enables us to understand agents.

Taking HADD in conjunction with ToM, it seems likely that belief about supernatural agents would emerge. Imagine, you are sitting on a boat in the middle of the ocean as you look up into the starry sky. It seems reasonable to think that the powerful experience of nature, given the aforementioned faculties, would result in the production of belief in a supernatural agent. Religious belief, then, is natural to human faculties. This, of course, does not mean that society does not play a role in believing in supernatural agents; nor does it mean that supernatural agents are not minimally counterintuitive.

When one states that religion is natural, one just means that basic human psychology plays a meaningful role in explaining religious belief. Barrett puts it as follows:

> The naturalness thesis is an attempt to push against the idea that religious expression is only the product of cultural factors and that basic human psychology makes no meaningful explanatory contribution, but not an attempt to claim that religious expression is nothing but the product of basic human psychology working in individualistic isolation. (Barrett, 2017, p. 126)

3.3 Wilkins and Griffiths' Debunking Argument

Initially, one might be inclined to think that CSR supports the thesis of Reformed epistemology. There seems to be empirical evidence for the *sensus divinitatis*. Humans possess a faculty aimed toward the production of theistic belief. Opponents of theistic belief have argued the very opposite.

John Wilkins and Paul Griffiths (2013) argue that, given naturalism and evolution, one should trust the reliability of their cognitive faculties, at least as it pertains to common-sense beliefs and beliefs derived from those common-sense beliefs. They argue for what they call the Milvian Bridge Principle.

> Milvian Bridge: X facts are related to the evolutionary success of X beliefs in such a way that it is reasonable to accept and act on X beliefs produced by our evolved cognitive faculties. (Wilkins and Griffiths, 2013, p. 134)

Roughly, the idea is that if belief that P is such that it aids in S's survival and reproductive behavior, then it's rational to accept P. For example, imagine that subject S is thirsty and needs water to survive. S would have to have a true belief about where the water was located in order to survive. The idea being, if S is consistently surviving based off of her beliefs about where the water is, her faculties as it pertains to the location of water should be seen as reliable. Similarly, suppose there is a mother who has several children that she is responsible for feeding. The mother would need to be able to correctly count both the portions of food that she fed her children and the number of children that she possessed in order for her and her progeny to meet the Darwinian requirement of survival and reproduction.

While Wilkins and Griffiths argue that there is a Milvian Bridge connection for common-sense beliefs, there is no Milvian Bridge–type connection for religious beliefs. Wilkins and Griffiths state, "If the 'hyperactive agency detection device' theory is correct, then people believe in supernatural agents which do not exist for the same reason that birds sometimes mistake harmless birds passing overhead for raptors" (Wilkins and Griffiths, 2013, p. 143). It is clear that Wilkins and Griffiths think that when it comes to religious beliefs, there is no tight connection between the belief produced and it being true. Thus, even if some religious belief turned out to be true, a subject still would not be warranted in thinking that the religious belief was true. They think that religious beliefs are "off-track" insofar as the process that produces the religious belief does not track truth, but rather "it produces beliefs in a manner that is insensitive to the truth of those beliefs" (Wilkins and Griffiths, 2013, p. 133).

Wilkins and Griffiths end up utilizing confirmation theory to argue that the probability of a specific religious belief being true is low, given that we would expect a subject to have religious belief even if the religious belief was false (Wilkins and Griffiths, 2013, pp. 143–144). We can see this point as a distinct one but related to the one articulated above. Having now engaged Wilkins and Griffiths' debunking argument, I move on to articulate Stephen Law's debunking argument.

3.4 Law's X-Argument

Law argues that HADD is responsible for humans believing in gods, ghosts, fairies, and psychic Sally (Law 2016). With HADD historically detecting agency in humans, even when agency is not there, can we reasonably trust beliefs about "hidden agents" that are the results of HADD functioning? Law thinks that we cannot. For him, there appears to be an undercutting defeater for belief in hidden agents. The probability, then, that one's belief about a hidden agent is true is low or perhaps inscrutable. In his "The X-claim argument against religious belief" (2016) (an X-claim is any claim that a person makes about an invisible agent), Law argues that the religious believer is in a situation analogous to that of the person in the snake hallucination scenario. The scenario goes as follows: "[S]uppose I seem to see a snake on the ground in front of me, and so come to believe there's a snake there. Then a reliable and trustworthy authority tells me that I have been given a drug that produces superrealistic visual snake hallucinations." According to Law, "many have the intuition that, given this new evidence, I can no longer be said to know there's a snake there" (Law, 2016, p. 19). However, Law himself does not make the claim that the religious believer would for sure lack warrant (though he seems sympathetic to this view); rather, the believer who reflects on Law's points would not be reasonable in thinking that the beliefs produced from HADD are true. The reflective believer has a rationality-undercutting defeater for her belief.

With the exception of the point made about confirmation theory by Wilkins and Griffiths, both debunking arguments are quite similar. Both arguments utilize that nature of HADD and argue from it that the beliefs it produces are not trustworthy. Wilkins and Griffiths argue that HADD is not trustworthy due to there being no connection between it and the survival of an organism. Law's argument focuses on the false positives that are produced from HADD in other individuals. What should the religious believer say? Is knowledge of God (or rational theistic belief) impossible for theists who reflect on these debunking arguments? I think not. Given that I think that Law's argument is stronger than Wilkins and Griffiths' argument, I will primarily address Law's argument, though my last two responses to Law can also be applied to Wilkins and Griffiths' argument. I will make this clear toward the end of the next section. I'll give two responses to Law. First, I will argue that if God exists (and the story that I give is true), then HADD is reliable with respect to producing general theistic or supernatural belief. Second, I will utilize a classic Plantingian response in showing how a subject's belief can be rational and warranted, despite there being propositional evidence against the belief in question.

3.5 General Reliability and the Classic Plantingian Response

Law claims that HADD, at least, with respect to "hidden agents" who possess "extraordinary power" is not reliable, for this mechanism is responsible for producing beliefs about ghosts, fairies, and psychics in various human beings. Overall though, the mechanisms involved (which include HADD) in producing belief about other agents are reliable. We come into contact with dozens and dozens of minds every day and it seems plausible that our faculties are doing a good job at achieving the right results about those agents. So, it seems that Law needs to do more work to explain why such faculties are reliable only when it comes to non-hidden agents.

This is especially so, given that if supernaturalism is true (at least the supernaturalism that I have described above), it would seem to follow that HADD is actually reliable. While it may be true that the faculty is not a reliable process with respect to specific supernatural beliefs, HADD would be reliable insofar as it gets agents aware of the supernatural or even, specifically, Divinity (Clark and Barrett, 2011). In this way of looking at HADD, God has given us a dim light of the heavenly reality, and there is room for our view of Divinity to grow and mature.

Perhaps this situation can be likened to a group of strangers who are in an extremely dark room. Each individual's faculties might produce false beliefs about what is in the room. However, there is a sense in which the faculties in question reliably produce the belief that there are objects in the room. The participants can then cooperate together to figure out what is actually in the room.[17] I imagine that there would be a certain trial-and-error process that would be implemented, basic principles of metaphysics and logic would be utilized, and each individual would need to trust certain individuals in the room and perhaps learn to not trust other individuals in the room; but eventually, it seems plausible that the individuals in the room could gain a general knowledge for what objects are in the dark room.[18] Upon reflection on Law's attempted undercutting defeater, if the theist is convinced that this is what is going on with respect to how religious beliefs are formed, I'm inclined to think that Law's X-argument will not amount to a defeater.

Let us assume this response does not satisfy Law. What is doing most of the work in Law's attempted defeater? I think it is the idea that the propositional evidence is such that the probability according to the sharable or objective evidence (what I will call the objective probability)[19] that one's religious belief is true, given the way HADD has produced false beliefs in other humans, is low. But the proper functionalist will likely think that the low objective probability of HADD being reliable is not sufficient to constitute a defeater. For a proper functionalist, non-propositional evidence can be such that, while the propositional evidence supports -P, the overall evidence still could support P. In fact, non-propositional evidence could be utilized to deflect undercutting defeaters. Michael Bergmann, for example, thinks the naturalist should appeal to non-propositional evidence as it pertains to deflecting Plantinga's Evolutionary Argument Against Naturalism. Bergmann states:

> Even if a naturalist believed that P(R/N&E) is low or inscrutable, this needn't give her a defeater for R. For she could have nonpropositional evidence for R that is sufficiently strong to make belief in R rational, reasonable, and warranted – even for someone whose total relevant propositional evidence, k, was such that P(R/k) is low or inscrutable. (Bergmann, 2002, p. 65)

---

[17] According to cognitive science of religion, group cooperation plays a fundamental role in religious belief formation. See Ara Norenzayan, *Big Gods – How Religion Transformed Cooperation and Conflict* (Princeton: Princeton University Press, 2015).

[18] Andrew Moon has suggested to me that this scenario is similar to Kai-Kwan's remnant example. See Kai-Kwan, "Can Religious Belief Provide Justification for Belief in God? The Debate in Contemporary Philosophy," *Philosophy Compass* 1/6 2006: 654.

[19] There are many ways to use the phrase "objective probability." By objective probability, I just mean what is probable given the evidence that is sharable or can be evaluated from a third-person perspective.

There are specific scenarios that help make this view more plausible. Elsewhere, inspired by Plantinga, I have given the following scenario:

> Say I am known for stealing philosophy books, in fact, there is even a picture of me, warning the clerks that I like to steal books. If, one day, the whole philosophy section of the library went missing and there were several witnesses saying they saw me steal a lot of books, the objective probability that I stole the books would be very high. Nonetheless, if I had a very distinct and highly warranted memory of myself at my house during the time that the books disappeared, would I have a defeater for my belief that I was at my house when the book snatching occurred? It doesn't appear to be the case that I would. As I hold to this belief with a sufficient amount of firmness (which is partly responsible for my level of warrant being high), the probability that I stole the philosophy books wouldn't play any significant role in my doxastic process. (Taber and McNabb, 2015, p. 7)

For a proper functionalist, the degree of warrant that a belief possesses depends on how firmly one holds to a proposition. Confidence that p is true helps determine whether a potential defeater can be deflected. If the religious believer entertains the attempted defeaters and is not significantly moved by them (her confidence is not shaken), then as long as her belief is the product of the aforementioned conditions, her belief is warranted. This can be the case given that, due to the proper functionalist constraints being in place, the subject's religious belief does not suffer from being relevantly lucky (McNabb and Baldwin, 2017, p. 301).

The proper functionalist then will likely endorse what I call the Classic Plantingian Approach (CPR).

> CPR: S's belief that p can deflect defeater D if S still believes p on the reflection of D and p is the product of properly functioning faculties which are successfully aimed at truth and there is a high objective probability [by objective probability, I don't mean it is probable given the objective or sharable evidence but that there is a likelihood of the belief being true in terms of frequency] that the belief produced under these conditions would be true. (McNabb and Baldwin, 2017, p. 301)

While a proper functionalist will not think that the probability given the evidence that is sharable or objective plays a significant role when determining what belief is rational to hold, there is still an important sense in which S's religious belief can still be seen as probable. It can be considered probable in terms of epistemic probability. Plantinga clarifies what one means by epistemic probability:

[T]o refer to the relationship between a pair of propositions A and B when A is evidence, propositional evidence, for B. More precisely, in those cases I shall say that the epistemic conditional probability of B on A is high ... Our question is: what is the relation between a pair of propositions A and B when the epistemic conditional probability of A on B is high? What kind of account or analysis can we give of this relation? What makes it the case that P(A/B) is high? (Plantinga 1993, p. 139)

Plantinga's account of epistemic probability goes as follows:

(CEP): P(A/B) = <x,y> iff <x,y> is the smallest interval which contains all of the intervals which represent the degree to which a rational human being S (for whom the conditions necessary for warrant hold) could believe A if she believed B, had no undercutting defeater for A, had no other source of warrant either for A or for –A, was aware that she believed B, and considered the evidential bearing of B on A. (Plantinga 1993, p. 168)

What is at the heart of epistemic probability is (1) S's belief that A is warranted given that she believes B, and (2) S lacks a defeater for A. Coming back to our concerns relating to CSR, if S's religious belief is warranted given that she believes that her specific belief-forming faculties are reliable, then S's epistemic probability that her religious belief is true would be high. Perhaps one does not think that it is possible that S could think that her specific belief-forming faculties (which include HADD) could be reliable given Law's argument. It might be the case, however, that S has an incredibly strong seeming that leads her to believe that her belief-forming faculties are reliable, even in light of Law's argument. This seeming would lead S to assign a high probability to the proposition that her faculties are reliable. And of course, if the seeming was produced from the proper functionalist constraints, she would be within her right to do so.

But what about the snake case? If the snake case was glossed in such a way that the subject was designed to produce the belief that there was a snake in front of her, even upon the reflection of taking hallucinogens, and there was a high statistical probability that the belief that there was a snake in front of her was true (given that it was produced from proper function conditions), the belief in question would be warranted. Initially, we are inclined to think that the belief in question would not amount to warrant because we think that her belief lacks a tight enough connection to the truth. However, once we gloss the scenario in such a way that the proper functionalist conditions are met, the intuitions will be different.

Notice, my last two points can be applied just as well to Wilkins and Griffiths' argument. If a religious believer reflects on their undercutting defeater and is not moved by it, assuming that her belief and confidence for her belief are produced by the proper functionalist constraints, the strength of her belief can deflect their defeater. And similarly, while it may be that according to the basic rules of confirmation theory, religious beliefs are not likely to be true, at least by way of only taking into account one's religious experience, S's religious beliefs could still be epistemically probable. And this is what the epistemologist should actually be concerned with.

Lastly, it is worth mentioning that both Law and Wilkins and Griffiths leave room for the religious believer to have warranted or rational religious belief by way of argument. In this case, it might be that S's religious belief is initially warranted by way of her religious experience; however, upon reflecting on one of the aforementioned debunking arguments, S's religious experience might not be enough to continue to allow S to be warranted or rational in her religious belief. S could, however, utilize resources from natural theology to help supplement her warrant for her religious belief. S, in this case, need not concede that her religious belief is defeated. I will now turn my attention to an epistemic argument that she could utilize. This argument will then help bridge the gap between epistemology and natural theology.

4 From Epistemology to Natural Theology

4.1 From Knowledge to God

In recent work, I have argued for the thesis of proper functionalism as it pertains to a theory of epistemic warrant (Baldwin and McNabb, forthcoming; McNabb, 2015). In addition to this, Erik Baldwin and I have argued that a worldview is not compatible with proper functionalism, unless the worldview in question is such that (1) it affirms the existence of a conscious and intentional designer, (2) whose nature and past actions are compatible with Plantinga's truth-aimed conditions, and (3) whose design plan for humans does not depend on or presuppose an actual infinite (McNabb and Baldwin, 2016; Baldwin and McNabb, forthcoming). Roughly, what we have shown is that knowledge, ultimately, is only compatible with something like a Judeo-Christian framework.

In this section, I develop and argue for a transcendental argument for God's existence. Specifically, I argue and defend the claim that since we have knowledge, God exists.[20] In order to defend this thesis, I will first reiterate the proper functionalist theory of warrant. Second, I will summarize the work that I have

---

[20] The argument in this section should not be confused with Jacek Wojtysiak's argument for God's existence, which is based on Plantinga's Evolutionary Argument Against Naturalism. See Jacek Wojtysiak, "Two Epistemological Arguments for the Existence of God," *European Journal of Philosophy of Religion* Vol. 10 (2018): 21–30.

done with Baldwin on proper functionalism as it relates to other world religions. Third, I will develop a transcendental argument for God's existence based on my previous work. Finally, I will entertain an objection from the Pyrrhonian tradition, which attempts to make implausible the claim that human beings possess knowledge.

4.2 Proper Functionalism

Again, the conditions of Plantinga's proper functionalist theory of warrant go as follows:

S's belief that P is warranted iff at the time S forms the belief that P,

1) S's cognitive faculties are functioning properly,
2) S's cognitive environment is sufficiently similar to the one for which S's cognitive faculties are designed,
3) The design plan that governs the production of beliefs is aimed at producing true belief, and
4) The design plan is a good one such that there is a high statistical (or objective) probability that a belief produced under these conditions will be true (Kim, 2011, p. 19).

Assuming that I have made proper functionalism plausible in Section 2 of this Element, the rest of this section will merely assume proper functionalism as the correct theory of warrant.

4.3 McNabb and Baldwin on the Preconditions of Proper Functionalism

As previously mentioned, Baldwin and I argue that in order for a worldview W to make full use of a proper functionalist theory of warrant, W needs to be such that:

(1) It affirms the existences of a conscious and intentional designer,
(2) whose nature and past actions are compatible with Plantinga's truth-aimed conditions, and
(3) whose design plan for humans does not depend on or presuppose there being an actual infinite (Baldwin and McNabb, forthcoming).

While it is intuitive to think that a design plan needs a designer, in our *Plantingian Religious Epistemology and World Religions*, we look at various non-theistic accounts of proper function to see if such accounts can account for the preconditions needed to make proper function intelligible. We start off with evolutionary accounts of proper function. Roughly, an evolutionary account of proper function goes as follows:

Faculty F functions properly, if F aids organism O in survival and reproduction, and, by way of acting in a similar fashion, F aided O's ancestors in survival and reproduction.[21]

Following Plantinga, we argue that these conditions for proper function are neither necessary nor sufficient (Plantinga and Tooley, 2008, pp. 24–28). The conditions are not necessary, for we can think of possible worlds where God exists and He creates people without ancestors; perhaps He even creates them instantaneously. These individuals would lack both ancestors and history, and yet it would seem right to think that their hearts or cognitive faculties are functioning properly (Plantinga and Tooley, 2008, p. 24).

Nor does it seem that these conditions are sufficient for proper function. Plantinga invites his readers to imagine a scenario where a Hitler-like madman and his regime inflict genetic harm on non-Aryans; perhaps the regime distorts and mutates the visual system of select non-Aryans (Plantinga and Tooley, 2008, p. 26). Even if the evil regime decided to kill the non-Aryan non-mutants for several generations to come, it would seem odd[22] to say that the later generations of non-Aryan mutants would have properly functioning visual systems. But, this is precisely what the evolutionary account would entail. The non-Aryan mutants would have visual systems that aid them in not getting killed off by the evil regime, and their visual systems would have aided their ancestors in the same way.[23]

In order to see if there are other non-theistic traditions that possess resources that would allow them to account for proper function in a way that naturalism cannot, we look at Advaita Vedanta Hinduism, Samkyha Hinduism, Mahayana Buddhism, Daoism, and The Learning of the Mind Neo-Confucian tradition. We end up arguing that these traditions lack the necessary resources to make sense of proper function. For example, we argue that the Advaita Vedanta and the Mahayana traditions cannot make sense of proper function, not only because one cannot make sense of a design plan, but also because one cannot make sense of faculties or design plans existing at all. For Advaita Vedanta

---

[21] For a precise evolutionary account, see Ruth Millikan, "In Defense of Proper Functions," *Philosophy of Science* 56 (1989): 288–289.

[22] See Erik Baldwin and Tyler Dalton McNabb, *Plantingian Religious Epistemology: Problems and Prospects* (Lanham: Lexington Press, forthcoming) for a more robust defense to this claim.

[23] In Erik Baldwin and Tyler Dalton McNabb, *Plantingian Religious Epistemology: Problems and Prospects* (Lanham: Lexington Press, forthcoming) we also take time to engage naturalistic Neo-Aristotelian accounts of proper function. Utilizing Aquinas's Fifth Way, we argue that one will not be able to make intelligible the ends of a faculty without a conscious designer. Thus, while there is a way to talk about proper function without directly appealing to God in Aristotelianism, we think, like Aquinas, that one will still indirectly need to appeal to God to make sense of proper function.

Hinduism, it is because, according to its doctrines, all that really exists in ultimate reality is the qualityless, impersonal Brahman (Harrison, 2012, p. 58). The Advaita Vedanta tradition then seems incompatible with a view that there are faculties that possess design plans. Similarly, according to the Mahayana Buddhist tradition, substance and permanence are illusory. Reality is ultimately empty and void (Nāgārjuna and Garfield, 1996, p. 98). Again, there is not much room for making sense of design plans or cognitive faculties on this view. They simply do not exist. We take it that the failure of such accounts helps confirm the initial intuition that a design plan needs a designer.

Later on in the work, we argue for condition (2) by way of engaging the Islamic tradition. Utilizing our paper "An Epistemic Defeater for Islamic Belief?" (Baldwin and McNabb, 2015), we reformulate Plantinga's Evolutionary Argument Against Naturalism and apply it to Islamic belief. The force of the argument is based on several instances that exist in the Koran where God both deceives and boasts about His ability to deceive. We use this paper to help highlight the importance of a tradition's depiction of the character of the designer of our cognitive faculties.

Finally, in our recent paper "Reformed Epistemology and the Pandora's Box Objection: The Vaisesika and Mormon Traditions"(McNabb and Baldwin, 2016), we point to both the Mormon and the orthodox Hindu traditions as traditions that assume the existence of an actual infinite insofar as explaining how the human design plan was constructed. For the former tradition, it seems to endorse that the designer of our cognitive faculties possesses cognitive faculties that likewise were designed by another designer, and that the other designer has faculties that were designed by another designer, *ad infinitum*. In reference to the latter tradition, the orthodox cosmology within Hinduism endorses that there has been an infinite amount of cosmological cycles that are responsible for shaping our cognitive faculties. Both Mormonism and orthodox Hinduism then tell stories about how human faculties have come about, which presuppose that there is an actual infinite.

We move from making these points to defending William Lane Craig's Infinity minus Infinity argument in arguing that an actual infinite is metaphysically impossible (Craig and Sinclair, 2009, p. 103). Roughly, the idea is that since you can subtract infinity from infinity and get conflicting answers, there is good reason to think that an actual infinity is not metaphysically possible. Defending this argument leads us to conclude that the Mormon and Hindu traditions cannot fully utilize Plantinga's epistemology, given that the traditions are committed to metaphysically impossible explanations for how human

faculties and design plans have come about. This again highlights the importance of a tradition depicting a metaphysically possible story for how our
human design plans came to be.

What becomes clear from our work is that not all worldviews can account for
the proper function of human faculties. In fact, it seems that a god who
resembles the Judeo-Christian tradition conception of God is a precondition
needed to make intelligible an account of proper function; and of course, with
that, a precondition needed to make intelligible the capacity for human
knowledge.

4.4 Transcendental Arguments

Typically, transcendental arguments in the contemporary literature are aimed at
disproving the thesis of skepticism. Often, advocates of transcendental arguments try to establish epistemic certainty with respect to the existence of an
external world or the existence of certain persons. However, this need not be the
only use of transcendental arguments. At the heart of a transcendental argument
is the idea that some preconditions can be accounted for only if a certain
proposition is true. Robert Stern summarizes it well in stating, "As standardly
conceived, transcendental arguments are taken to be distinctive in involving a
certain sort of claim, namely that X is a necessary condition for the possibility
of Y – where then, given that Y is the case, it logically follows that X must be the
case too."[24] And it is within this respect that I want to propose the following
argument:

(1) If God does not exist, human beings cannot possess knowledge.
(2) Human beings do possess knowledge.

   Therefore,

(3) God exists.

Without being able to engage our work in detail, for purposes of this section I
will assume that our work described above makes (1) more plausible than its
negation. This would just leave (2). (2) can be made plausible by an epistemic
seeming. It surely appears to be the case that humans have knowledge. It
appears to me that I know that I am writing this Element, or that I know that
there are other minds around me, or that 2 plus 2 is 4, or that it is wrong to
mutilate people for fun. Of course, just because it appears to be the case, it does
not necessarily follow that it is the case. However, if we take an innocent-until-

---

[24] Robert Stern, "Transcendental Arguments," *Internet Encyclopedia of Philosophy*, www.iep
.utm.edu/trans-ar.

proven-guilty stance with our seemings (a stance that fits nicely with proper functionalism), those who have a strong seeming and see seemings as evidence for (2) should affirm (2) until it is clear that there are defeaters for it.

But are there such defeaters? I'm inclined to think there are not. In fact, given the psychological certainty I have for affirming (2), I am uncertain as to what it would take to defeat (2). Historically speaking, other philosophers have not shared my attitude. Specifically, there are attempted defeaters from the Pyrrhonian tradition that philosophers, even currently, take very seriously. I'd like to take a representative argument from this tradition and contend that the argument fails to establish the thesis of skepticism. In doing this, I hope to defend (2) and thus make it even more plausible.

4.5 Pyrrhonian Skepticism

Following Jonathan Barnes, Ernest Sosa lays out the methodological process of the Pyrrhonian tradition as follows:

(A) Modes (i.e., the arguments from skepticism) lead to isosthenia (equipollence).
(B) Isosthenia leads to epoche (suspension of judgment).
(C) Epoche leads to ataraxia (tranquility).
(D) Ataraxia is fundamental to eudaemonia (flourishing) (Sosa, 2015, p. 216; cf. Barnes, 1982, pp. 2–3).[25]

The idea, for the Pyrrhonist, is that arguments that can establish skepticism will force a subject to rationally suspend judgement as to whether a proposition is true. The suspension of the judgment leads to tranquility, and once a subject reaches a state of tranquility, she will be able to flourish. While the Pyrrhonian tradition contains an overall philosophy for how a subject ought to run their life, I will ignore the overall philosophy and focus specifically on a representative argument or mode from the tradition that is used to establish skepticism.

4.6 Agrippa's Trilemma Revisited

As discussed in Section 1, when one asks a subject, S, why she believes that P, S will offer a reason, r1, that she thinks justifies her belief that P. One can then continue to ask S why she believes r1, and S would give reason r2. This questioning can go on *ad infinitum*, stop at a final reason, or circle back to r1.

---

[25] Jonathan Barnes, "The Beliefs of a Pyrrhonist," in E. J. Kenny and M. M. MacKenzie eds., *Proceedings of the Cambridge Philosophical Society* (Cambridge: Cambridge University Press, 1982).

Continuing to assume the truth of the proper functionalist thesis for purposes of this section, one should be committed to foundationalism and thus endorse the first of the aforementioned options. Foundationalists think that basic beliefs are the bedrock of our knowledge and thus one cannot give any further reason for why a basic belief is justified. Peter Klein takes issue with foundationalists, however. He thinks that human knowledge is incompatible with the foundationalist response. Foundationalism, according to Klein, entails that one rejects that rational beliefs are necessary for human knowledge. Klein states, "Thus, if having rational beliefs is a necessary condition of some type of knowledge, both foundationalism and coherentism lead directly to the consequence that this type of knowledge is not possible." (Klein, 1999, p. 298)

In arguing for this claim, Klein endorses two principles that he sees as eminently plausible:

> Principle of Avoiding Circularity (PAC): For all x, if a person, S, has a justification for x, then for all of y, if y is in the evidential ancestry of x for S, then x is not in the evidential ancestry of y for S. (Klein, 1999, p. 298)

> Principle of Avoiding Arbitrariness (PAA): For all x, if a person, S, has a justification for x, then there is some reason R1, available to S for x; and there is some reason r2, available to S for R1; etc. (Klein, 1999, p. 299)

According to Klein:

> Some foundationalists could accept PAA by claiming that the available reason, r, could just be x, itself. They could assert that some propositions are "self-justified." That is not ruled out by PAA; but coupled with PAC, that possibility is ruled out. Indeed, the combination of PAC and PAA entails that the evidential ancestry of a justified belief be infinite and non-repeating. Thus, someone wishing to avoid infinitism must reject either PAC or PAA (or both). (Klein, 1999)

Since most epistemologists will not want to reject PAC due to wanting to avoid circularity, Klein thinks the foundationalist is going to want to reject PAA. Agreeing with Klein, I now turn to defending a specifically proper functionalist rejection of PAA.

Klein entertains the possibility of someone rejecting PAA for reliabilist (a close cousin to a proper functionalist) considerations. There are certain beliefs, for the moderate reliabilist, that do not need reasons at all. As long as the belief is reliably produced (at least, for the process reliabilist), the belief can constitute knowledge. But Klein rejects that such knowledge should be considered "human knowledge." Rather, he quotes Sosa in arguing that at best, such an account would be to establish animal knowledge, which for Klein, is not adequate. Human knowledge is on a much "higher plane" (Klein, 1999, p. 302). Given that proper functionalism and reliabilism are so closely related, I think it is safe to assume that we can replace reliabilism with proper functionalism and Klein would still endorse the stated consequence.

So, what are we to do with the claim that animal knowledge is significantly inferior to human knowledge? The proper functionalist thinks that it is the design plan that dictates when a belief needs reasons to ground it and when the belief can be held rationally apart from reasons. For example, it might be that the design plan does not require that a subject have access to the properties that confer warrant for the belief in other minds. That is to say, the design plan could be such that with respect to belief in other minds, S can be rational in holding to this belief, even if S is without sufficiently good reasons to believe it. However, it might require that a subject have access to some of the properties that confer warrant for other beliefs that the subject holds, such as in the case of belief in the correct theory of warrant or belief in the correct interpretation of quantum mechanics.

If what I have argued for thus far is right, the proper functionalist should not think that her foundational beliefs should be considered as an inferior form of knowledge in comparison to beliefs that are based on reasons. Again, take the belief in other minds as an example. Subject S will have some sort of experience or phenomenological happening that leads her to affirm that there are other minds, and the belief in question has a high statistical probability of being true, given that it is produced from the proper functionalist constraints. The proper functionalist will not see why reason-based knowledge should be seen as significantly superior to non–reason-based knowledge. Both knowledge without reasons and knowledge with reasons are the result of a design plan that is ultimately grounded in the intentions of a designer. The designer could have made it such that belief in the correct theory of warrant did not require reasons for its justification, while the design plan would have required that we have such reasons in order to be justified in our belief about other minds.

Perhaps there are other reasons for thinking that reason-based knowledge is far superior to non–reason-based knowledge. Max Baker-Hytch, for example, argues that animal knowledge is deficient for at least two reasons (Baker-Hytch, 2018, p. 199). First, it is deficient because reason-based knowledge, or as he (following Ernest Sosa) calls it, reflective knowledge, can be easily possessed by a subject. Baker-Hytch clarifies what he means in the following way:

> Typically, it is very easy to know that a perceptual belief is an item of knowledge, for instance. What is the process by which we form second-order beliefs about whether our perceptual beliefs are knowledge? Presumably it is some kind of default disposition to assume that things are going normally with our perceptual systems unless there are internally

accessible indicators that things are going awry – indicators such as a failure of various sensory impressions to cohere fully with one another, reports of an event by other people that conflict with the deliverances of one's own senses concerning that event, memories of having been exposed to substances that one knows to have an adverse effect on perception, and so on (Baker-Hytch, 2018, p. 199).

Second, Baker-Hytch argues that animal knowledge is deficient because, assuming that knowledge is the norm of assertion, animal knowledge would not be sufficient to assert that one knows that one's religious beliefs are true (Baker-Hytch, 2018, p. 200). Even if it could be said from an objective observer's position that a subject does in fact know that God exists, the subject would not know that she knows that God exists, and therefore the subject could still be criticized for asserting that God exists since she claims something that she does not know that she can permissibly claim.

I am not convinced that these should be considered sufficient reasons for thinking that animal knowledge is significantly deficient. Taking Baker-Hytch's second point first, Baker-Hytch recognizes that philosophy is a controversial domain that makes it hard to know whether one has knowledge of a controversial philosophical claim. His response to this, however, is to argue that there is a way to hedge assertions in such a way that exempts a speaker from violating the norm of assertion. Baker-Hytch does not think this can be said of subjects who possess only animal knowledge. He states, "By contrast, Kane's religion exhorts her to proclaim the contents of her beliefs. And proclamation, I take it, involves outright assertion rather than assertion which is hedged or somehow softened so as to be exempt from the knowledge norm" (Baker-Hytch, 2018).

While it is true that much of philosophy is done in such a way as to not actually state that something is the case, nonetheless there is still a lot of philosophy that is done that makes claims about what is the case. For example, libertarians about free will (Kane, 2005) often argue that in order to be responsible with respect to a particular action, a subject must have the ability to do otherwise. Rawlsians (Rawls, 2005) typically tell us what justice actually is. And Swinburnians (Swinburne, 2014) tell us that it is more likely than not that God exists (sometimes by way of giving an extremely precise calculation). So, it seems that Hytch-Baker's view that knowledge is the norm of assertion, and that one cannot permissibly claim p unless one knows that one knows that p, has an extremely negative effect on the field of philosophy. Moreover, is Hytch-Baker's view a controversial philosophical view? Surely it is. Furthermore, does Hytch-Baker know that he knows that his norm principle is true? If not, Hytch-Baker likewise should not assert it.

Regarding Baker-Hytch's first point, I think there is a tension in his work. On one hand, he seems too optimistic about how easy it is to have second-order knowledge. On the other hand, he recognizes that for most controversial philosophical assertions, philosophers should not outright assert a view, but hedge their assertions to make them acceptable such that they do not violate the norm of assertion. So which one is it? I'm inclined to think that at the metalevel, there are certain beliefs that we will have to take as circular, and as I have argued elsewhere, there is nothing epistemically wrong with that.[26] Having said all of this, I fail to see why one should view animal knowledge or non–reason-based knowledge as significantly deficient.[27]

4.7 The Metalevel and Foundationalism

I have been arguing that in responding to the PAA principle, the proper functionalist should resort to metalevel analysis, specifically, an analysis rooted in the proper functionalist constraints in order to show that their beliefs are not arbitrary. Klein not only rejects this move from externalists, for reasons considered above, but he also argues that an appeal to metalevel analysis (or what he calls metalevel justification)[28] does not work for the following reason. Klein states that "either metalevel justification provides a reason for thinking the base proposition is true (and hence regress does not end) or it does not (hence accepting the base proposition is arbitrary). The Pyrrhonians are right" (Klein, 1990). Klein thinks that the foundationalist will appeal to causal processes or history in order to show that their belief is likely true. And upon doing so, they open themselves up to being

---

[26] For more on this, see Tyler Dalton McNabb, "Proper Functionalism and the Metalevel: A Friendly Response to Timothy and Lydia McGrew," *Quaestiones Disputatae* 8/2 (2018): 155–164.

[27] For argument's sake, let's assume that, at best, the proper functionalist can only account for humans possessing animal knowledge and not human knowledge. Does Klein's argument defeat (2)?

I think not. If the proper function condition is a necessary condition for animal knowledge, the proper functionalist still has a syllogism that she can offer:

(1) If God does not exist, human beings cannot possess animal knowledge.
(2) Human beings do possess animal knowledge.

Therefore,

(3) God exists.

(1) would still depend on the work discussed at the beginning of this section. And the plausibility of (2) would largely depend on a seeming as well as the ability to show that there are no defeaters for it. The only difference between this argument and the one presented earlier is that this argument refers to animal knowledge while the former assumes knowledge on a "higher plane." The conclusion remains the same; humans possess knowledge (of some sort), so God exists.

[28] By metalevel justification, Klein just means justification designed to explain how certain beliefs are justified apart from reasons. See Peter Klein, "Human Knowledge and the Infinite Regress of Reasons," *Philosophical Perspectives* 13 (1999): 303–304.

questioned about their reason for thinking that their metalevel justification makes it such that their object level belief is likely true. Of course, if they do not want to appeal to metalevel justification, then their belief should be seen as arbitrary.

But as Michael Bergmann has pointed out, foundationalists are not appealing to metalevel justification to show why their object level belief is likely true, but rather, "the foundationalist is using the ideas in that meta-justificatory argument to explain why it is that lacking a reason for a belief is not sufficient for that belief's being arbitrary. The aim is to avoid arbitrariness, not by providing a reason for b, but by casting doubt on an assumption about what is sufficient for b's being arbitrary" (Bergmann, 2004, pp. 164–165).

And because of this, I fail to feel the force of Klein's argument. It seems that a foundationalist can appeal to externalist considerations for thinking that the beliefs she has are not arbitrary,[29] and it seems that her beliefs, which are not held on the basis of sufficiently good reasons, can still constitute knowledge that is worthy to be called human knowledge. The Pyrrhonian-inspired objection, then, seems to miss the mark. Therefore, I think we should regard (2) of the syllogism offered in this section as more plausible than not. What follows from this, then, is that since humans possess knowledge, God exists.

4.8 Conclusion

I first began this Element by way of laying out my thesis. Roughly, I said I would be arguing for Plantinga's religious epistemology. This led me to first survey several contemporary religious epistemologies. I briefly argued that these epistemologies, by themselves, were ultimately not satisfactory. I then introduced Plantinga's proper functionalism and argued for it. This allowed me to then argue for the thesis of Reformed epistemology. However, Plantinga's religious epistemology is not immune from objections. Thus, I spent Section 3 arguing that debunking arguments from cognitive science are not a threat to Plantinga's religious epistemology. Finally, I utilized Plantinga's epistemology to formulate an argument for God's existence. In this way, we have breached a gap between religious epistemology and natural theology.

---

[29] Perhaps while there is a sense that, externally, the foundationalist's beliefs are not arbitrary (e.g., the beliefs are produced from properly functioning faculties), there is an internalist sense in which the foundationalist's beliefs could still be considered arbitrary. The externalist of course is not likely to have the intuition that internal arbitrariness is troubling. Whether she should be concerned is a question for another time.

References

Baker-Hytch, M. (2018). Testimony amidst diversity. In M. A. Benton, J. Hawthorne, and D. Rabinowitz, eds., *Knowledge, Belief, and God New Insights in Religious Epistemology*. Oxford: Oxford University Press, pp. 183–202.

Baldwin, E., & McNabb, T. D. (2015). An epistemic defeater for Islamic belief? *International Journal of Philosophy and Theology*, **76**(4), 352–67.

(Forthcoming). *Plantingian Religious Epistemology: Problems and Prospects*, Lanham: Lexington Press.

Barrett, J. L. (2011). *Cognitive Science, Religion, and Theology: From Human Minds to Divine Minds*, PA: Templeton Press.

(2017). Religion is kid stuff: Minimally counterintuitive concepts are better remembered by young people. In R. G. Hombeck, J. L. Barrett, & M. Kang, eds., *Religious Cognition in China: "Homo Religiosus" and the Dragon*. Cham: Springer International Publishing, pp. 125–37.

Bergmann, M. (2002). Common sense naturalism. In J. Beilby, ed., *Naturalism Defeated? Essays on Plantinga's Evolutionary Argument Against Naturalism*. Ithaca: Cornell University Press, pp. 61–90.

(2004). What's NOT wrong with foundationalism. *Philosophy and Phenomenological Research*, **LXVIII**(1), 164–5.

BonJour, L. (1985). *The Structure of Empirical Knowledge*. Cambridge, MA: Harvard University Press.

Boyce, K., & Moon, A. (2016). In defense of proper functionalism: cognitive science takes on Swampman. *Synthese*, **123**(9), 2987–3001.

Boyce, K., & Plantinga, A. (2012). Proper functionalism. In A. Cullison, ed., *Companion to Epistemology*. Continuum Press, pp. 124–40.

Casler, K., & Kelemen, D. (2008). Developmental continuity in teleo-functional explanation: Reasoning about nature among Romanian Romani adults. *Journal of Cognition and Development*, **9**(3), 340–62.

Clark, K. J., & Barrett, J. L. (2011). Reidian religious epistemology and the cognitive science of religion. *Journal of the American Academy of Religion*, **79**(3), pp. 639–75.

Craig, W. L., and Sinclair, James. (2009). The kalam cosmological argument. In W. L. Craig and J. P. Moreland, eds., *The Blackwell Companion to Natural Theology*. Malden, UK: Blackwell Publishing, pp. 101–201.

Davidson, D. (1987). Knowing one's own mind. *Proceedings and Addresses of the American Philosophical Association*, **60**(3), 441–58.

DePoe, J. (2013). In defense of classical foundationalism: A critical evaluation of Plantinga's argument that classical foundationalism is self-refuting. *South African Journal of Philosophy*, 245–51.

(Forthcoming). Classical evidentialism. In J. DePoe and T. Dalton, eds., *Debating Religious Epistemology: An Introduction to Five Views on the Knowledge of God*. New York: Bloomsbury Press.

Feldman, R. (1985). Reliability and justification. *The Monist*, **68**:**2**, 159–74.

Gage, L., & McAllister, B. (Forthcoming). The phenomenal conservative approach to religious epistemology. In J. DePoe and T. Dalton, eds., *Debating Religious Epistemology: An Introduction to Five Views on the Knowledge of God*. NY: Bloomsbury Press.

Goldman, A. (1992). *Philosophy Meets the Cognitive and Social Sciences*. Cambridge, MA: MIT Press.

Gettier, E. (1963). Is justified true belief knowledge? *Analysis*, **23** (6), 121–3.

Guthrie, S. E. (1993). *Faces in the Clouds: A New Theory of Religion*. New York: Oxford University Press.

Harrison, V. (2012). *Eastern Philosophy: The Basics*. London: Routledge.

Järnefelt, E., Canfield, C. F., & Kelemen, D. (2015). The divided mind of a disbeliever: intuitive beliefs about nature as purposefully created among different groups of non-religious adults. *Cognition*, **140**, 72–88.

Kane, R. (2005). *A Contemporary Introduction to Free Will*. Oxford: Oxford University Press.

Kelemen, D. (1999). Why are rocks pointy? Children's preference for teleological explanations of the natural world. *Developmental Psychology*, **35**(6), 1440–52.

Kelemen, D., & Rosset, E. (2009). The human function compunction: teleological explanation in adults. *Cognition*, **111**(1), 138–43.

Kelly, T. (2005). The epistemic significance of disagreement. In J. Hawthorne, ed., *Oxford Studies in Epistemology*. Oxford: Oxford University Press, pp. 167–96.

(2010). Peer disagreement and higher order evidence. In R. Feldman and T. Warfield, eds., *Disagreement*. New York: Oxford University Press, pp. 111–74.

Kim, J. (2011). *Reformed Epistemology and the Problem of Religious Diversity: Proper Function, Epistemic Disagreement, and Christian Exclusivism*. Eugene, OR: Pickwick Publications.

Klein, P. (1999). Human knowledge and the infinite regress of reasons. *Philosophical Perspectives*, **13**(s13), 297–325.

Kundert, C., & Edman, L. R. O. (2017). Testing naturalness theory hypothesis in China. In R. G. Hombeck, J. L. Barrett, and M. Kang, eds., *Religious*

Cognition in China: "Homo Religiosus" and the Dragon. Cham: Springer International Publishing, pp. 77–97.

Kwan, K. (2006). Can religious belief provide justification for belief in God? The debate in contemporary philosophy. *Philosophy Compass*, 1(6), 640–61.

Law, S. (2016). The X-claim argument against religious belief. *Religious Studies*, **54**(1), 15–35.

Lehrer, K. (1965). Knowledge, truth, and evidence. *Analysis*, 25(5), 168–75.

McGrew, T. & McGrew, L. (2006). *Internalism and Epistemology: The Architecture of Reason*. London: Routledge Press.

McNabb, T. D. (2015). Warranted religion: answering objections to Alvin Plantinga's epistemology. *Religious Studies*, **51**(4), 477–95.

McNabb, T. D., & Baldwin, E. (2016). Reformed epistemology and the Pandora's box objection: the Vaisesika and Mormon traditions. *Philosophia Christi*, **18**(2), 451–65.

(2017). Divine methodology: a lawful deflection of Kantian and Kantian-esque defeaters. *Open Theology*, **3**(1), 293–304.

Millikan, R. (1989). In defense of proper functions. *Philosophy of Science*, 56(2), 288–9.

Moon, A. (2016). Recent work in reformed epistemology. *Philosophy Compass*, **11**(12), 879–91.

(2018). How to use cognitive faculties you never knew you had. *Pacific Philosophical Quarterly*, **99**(s1), 251–75.

Nāgārjuna, & Garfield, J. (1996). *Fundamental Wisdom of the Middle Way: Nāgārjuna's 'mulamadhymakakarika' with a Philosophical Commentary*. Oxford: Oxford University Press.

Norenzayan, A. (2015). *Big Gods – How Religion Transformed Cooperation and Conflict*. Princeton: Princeton University Press.

Plantinga, A. (1993). *Warrant and Proper Function*. New York: Oxford University Press.

(2000). *Warranted Christian Belief*. New York: Oxford University Press.

Plantinga, A., & Tooley, M. (2008). *Knowledge of God*. MA: Blackwell Publishing.

Pritchard, D. (2012). *Epistemological Disjunctivism*. Oxford: Oxford University Press.

Rawls, J. (2005). *A Theory of Justice*. Oxford: Oxford University Press.

Reid, T. (1983). Essay on the intellectual powers of man. In R. Beanblossom and K. Lehrer, eds., *Thomas Reid's Inquiry and Essays*. IN: Hackett, pp. 281–2.

Rottman, J., Zhu, L., Wang, W., Schillaci, R. S., Clark, K. J., and Kelemen, D. (2017) Cultural Influences on the teleological stance: Evidence from

China. *Religion, Brain and Behavior*, **7**(1) 17–26. doi: 10.1080/2153599X.2015.1118402.

Shaw, K. (2016). Religious disjunctivism. *International Journal of Philosophy of Religion*, **79**(3), 261–79.

Smith, M. (2014). The epistemology of religion. *Analysis*, **74**(1), 135–47.

Sosa, E. (2015). Judgement and Agency. Oxford: Oxford University Press.

(1991). *Knowledge in Perspective*. Cambridge: Cambridge University Press.

(1996). Proper functionalism and virtue epistemology. In J. L. Kvanvig, ed., *Warrant in Contemporary Epistemology: Essays in Honor of Plantinga's Theory of Knowledge*. MD: Rowman & Littlefield Publishers, pp. 258–59.

Swinburne, R. (2014). *The Existence of God*. Oxford: Oxford University Press.

Taber, T., & McNabb, T. (2015). Is the problem of divine hiddenness a problem for the reformed epistemologist? *The Heythrop Journal*, **57**(6).

Tolly, J. (Forthcoming). Swampman: A dilemma for proper functionalists. Synthesis.

Wilkins, J. S., & Griffiths, P. E. (2013). Evolutionary debunking arguments in three domains: fact, value, and religion. In J. Maclaurin and G. Dawes, eds., *A New Science of Religion*. London: Routledge, pp. 133–46.

Wright, S. (2013). Does Klein's infinitism offer a response to Agrippa's Trilemma? *Synthese*, **190**(6), 1113–30.

Acknowledgments

I want to thank Michael Devito for his friendship and feedback. I also want to thank Andrew Moon for some of his comments on Section 3. Finally, I want to thank my wife (Priscilla) and my children (Eden, Elijah, Ezra, and Eva-Maria) for allowing me to spend time on this project.

Cambridge Elements ≡

Philosophy of Religion

Yujin Nagasawa
University of Birmingham

Yujin Nagasawa is Professor of Philosophy and Co-Director of the John Hick Centre for Philosophy of Religion at the University of Birmingham. He is currently President of the British Society for the Philosophy of Religion. He is a member of the Editorial Board of *Religious Studies*, the *International Journal for Philosophy of Religion* and *Philosophy Compass*.

About the Series

This Cambridge Elements series provides concise and structured introductions to all the central topics in the philosophy of religion. It offers balanced, comprehensive coverage of multiple perspectives in the philosophy of religion. Contributors to the series are cutting-edge researchers who approach central issues in the philosophy of religion. Each provides a reliable resource for academic readers and develops new ideas and arguments from a unique viewpoint.

Cambridge Elements ≡

Philosophy of Religion

Elements in the Series

A full series listing is available at: www.cambridge.org/EPREL

Made in the USA
Las Vegas, NV
11 January 2021

15756991R00033